Signs and Wonders in the Last Days

Jay E. Adams

MID-AMERICA
INSTITUTE FOR NOUTHETIC STUDIES

Institute for Nouthetic Studies, a ministry of Mid-America Baptist
Theological Seminary, 5640 Airline Road, Arlington, TN 38002
mabts.edu and nouthetic.org

ISBN: 978-1-970445-07-7 (Print)
ISBN: 978-1-970445-08-4 (eBook)
Old ISBN: 978-1-889032-19-0

Editor: Donn R. Arms

Library of Congress Cataloging-in-Publication Data
Names: Adams, Jay E., 1929 - 2020
Title: *Signs and Wonders in the Last Day*
by Jay E. Adams
Description: Arlington, TN: Institute for Nouthetic Studies, 2025
Identifiers: ISBN 9781970445077 (paper)
Classification: LCC BT821.2 .A18 | DDC 234.13

Published in the United States of America

Table of Contents

INTRODUCTION

PERHAPS it seems strange to you that someone as deeply involved in counseling and preaching as I am would be writing a book like this. But let me explain. If you are doing psychological counseling, of course you'd never think of such an enterprise. But I have been doing and teaching *biblical* preaching and counseling. My counseling has grown out of extensive exegetical work, the fruit of which I have applied to life's problems. In contrast to the type of biblical theological preaching that focuses on the indicative to the neglect (or total absence) of the imperative, I have taught and practiced edificational preaching which is designed to change lives. As a result, that approach to counseling and preaching has continually brought me into intimate contact with the biblical text.[1]

Because I have continually come up against the problems of exegesis, interpretation, exposition, and application, over the years I have developed what I believe to be an approach to the Scriptures that does justice to the original intent of the Holy Spirit and, at the same time, solves some of the problems that to this point have not been adequately addressed. I wish, therefore, to share this approach with others. When you grapple with the difficulties that counselees present, when you struggle to apply a text in preaching in an accurate and relevant manner to those assembled before you, or when you simply want to understand God's Word for yourself, you must devote much thinking to the sort of matters that I deal with in this book.

Moreover, in counseling and in the pastoral ministry—as well as in teaching at two seminaries—I have been constantly confront-

---

1   That is why I have translated the New Testament, Psalm 119, Proverbs and Ecclesiastes and written commentaries on these books.

ed with gross misinterpretations of the Scriptures by both laymen and students, and with the numerous errors and even heresies that result therefrom. You may try to sidestep these issues, avoiding them as much as possible, but as a leader in Christ's church, you will rarely help others if you do (I do not mention the harm that error will do to you). In the endeavor to bring the pure Word of God into the lives of counselees, students, and members of congregations, I have had to study the Scriptures carefully from the perspective of *how the Bible itself insists that it must be interpreted and used.* It is not proper to impose some system upon the Scriptures from the outside, as many do. What we need is a clear understanding of how God directs us *in* the Bible to understand and apply the divine revelation that it is. To handle this revelation properly, nothing less than divine directives and examples, prayerfully used, are needed.

In addition, the biblical expositor and teacher, in his endeavor to be true to the Scriptures, is thrown up against the problems with which this book deals. These matters are not merely of superficial or esoteric interest to him; they are of a very basic nature, matters of concern in almost everything that he does. His work, his life, and his ability to teach others are dependent upon getting them right.

Finally, because it has always been my desire to help fledgling preachers and counselors succeed in their tasks, and because I have spent much of my ministry providing help and direction to them so as to facilitate their tasks, I am happy to present what I believe to be a point of view that will enhance both the understanding and the preaching of God's revelation. I can think of few contributions to such activities that would be of greater significance to the causes in which I believe.

These are some of the reasons why I have written this book. If it keeps men from going astray as so many good (but gullible) men have, if it guides others around the many pitfalls of interpretation, if it provides a framework for correct understanding and exposition of the Bible, I will be gratified and conclude that my efforts have not been in vain.

But what sorts of problems will I address? What kinds of errors will be refuted? They are of various sorts. Some have to do with eschatology. For example, there are those who claim that Jesus and the apostles thought that the second coming was imminent in their day and were simply mistaken. These critics have not been satisfactorily answered. To say as a reply that the "last days" refers to the entire New Testament period, as many do, hardly satisfies those who think clearly. "This generation," for instance, does not mean a time period over 2000 years long! That response certainly doesn't honor the New Testament writers' expectations as they expressed them in the pages of the New Testament. There must be a better answer. I have set forth that answer in this volume.

In addition, to say that the many signs and wonders that accompanied the apostles have ceased is a common assertion among conservatives, but the explanations they give for this position are usually so disappointing that the charismatic continues to have a field day. This book offers a conclusive argument against the idea of the continuation of special spiritual gifts.

"But these things all seem disconnected," you say. "What in the world is this book dealing with anyway? If I continue to read, what will I be reading about?"

The question is understandable. What I am addressing here is not merely one subject or another. It is an understanding of the New Testament that sweeps across many landscapes. It involves a way of coming to the books of the New Testament that has much to do with interpretation that reaches into all sorts of doctrinal and practical areas. Dispensationalism, for instance, is an understanding of the Bible that influences how you look at and apply nearly every passage you interpret. Though not as all-inclusive as dispensationalism, what I present here does something similar for large portions of the New Testament. It is, I know, difficult to fathom how this can be simply by speaking about the matter. So, let us turn to the study itself to see what I mean.

CHAPTER 1

WHAT SORTS OF PROBLEMS ARE THERE?

B EFORE over viewing the contents of the book or diving into specific matters in depth, it is important to understand the kind of errors in biblical interpretation and application that occasioned this book. But even before that, I urge you not to get lost in any of the particular problems that we shall be confronting throughout, only to miss the main point. It is possible that you may disagree with me concerning specifics in ways that do not affect the overall thrust of the book. Please keep this in mind, if you can, so as to benefit from the basic approach to the New Testament that is offered. I am convinced that the sort of issues I deal with are too seldom raised, let alone answered. So don't miss the forest while pressing your nose up against the bark of some tree.

The sorts of errors that I refute all have to do with ways of using the Bible that, according to its own usage and testimony, are proven to be fallacious. These errors result from approaching all the passages of the New Testament as if they may be applied to us today directly in a one-for-one matching pattern, even though they had their primary application to other periods, places, and people under very different circumstances. Passages that apply to us only in a secondary way (no less authoritatively or significantly, you understand, but, nevertheless, differently) must not be applied as though there were no difference. It is those differences that, in fact, make all the difference.

Let's take an example of what I am talking about. In Acts 4 we see the persecuted disciples released from prison, but laboring still under the threat of further imprisonment. They pray for boldness so that they may preach effectively. In response, God (literally) shakes the room, and the Holy Spirit instantly comes upon them in a special manner that makes them even bolder than they were before, so that they can speak God's Word properly before the persecuting authorities. Jim Cymbala, referring to this particular occasion in Acts 4 and applying it to us today, without any sort of understanding or mention of the special promises that had been made to the apostles, *as* apostles, or of the special times in which they ministered, in a widely-touted book writes: "This is the church on the move, giving us a Spirit-inspired model for today."[11] That statement is as irresponsible as it is untrue. There is no such *model* for us today. The apostles were told previously by the Lord Jesus Christ that when they were persecuted, they would receive peculiar power to speak without preparation by the Holy Spirit's enabling. In Acts 4, there is a specific fulfillment of our Lord's clear promises, which were as follows:

> *But when they deliver you up, don't worry about what you will say or how you will say it, because what you must say will be given to you in that hour. You aren't the ones who will be speaking, but the Spirit of My Father speaking in you.*
>
> (Matthew 10:19-20)[2]

> *Now when they arrest you and bring you to trial, don't worry before-hand about what you will say. Rather, say whatever is given to you in that hour (it won't be you speaking, but the Holy Spirit).*
>
> (Mark 13:11)

> *Now, when they bring you before synagogs and rulers and authori-ties, don't worry about what you will say in defense or how to do so, because the Holy Spirit will teach you in that very hour what you ought to say.*   (Luke 12:11-12)

---

1   Jim Cymbala, *Fresh Wind, Fresh Fire* (Grand Rapids: Zondervan, 1977), p. 94.

2   Indeed, as Matthew 10:1 and 11:1 indicate, the entire tenth chapter was spoken to the disciples, and to them alone, about the unique ministry they would be carrying on.

Get it settled in your hearts not to practice your defense beforehand, because I will give you words and wisdom that none of your opponents will be able to withstand or contradict. (Luke 21:14-15)

I have shown elsewhere that this promise included even the ability to speak by inspiration, so that all that the apostles said would be inerrant.[3] The boldness for which they prayed was *parresia*, a Greek word used throughout the book of Acts to describe apostolic preaching. It differs from the common word for boldness in that it doesn't refer to daring activity in general, but to the courage to *speak* without reservation or fear of consequences. It was in fulfillment of the promises of the Lord Jesus that this special coming of the Spirit upon the apostles, heralded by the miraculous shaking, took place. Those promises were not made to us today; they were the *special* prerogative of *special* persons living in the apostolic age.

So to say without qualification that this passage is a *model* for us today, as Cymbala does, clearly is misleading. The only legitimate sense in which we might use it as a model today would be in a *secondary* sense. Some of the principles involved certainly apply to us. We, too, need boldness to speak. We, too, should pray for such boldness; we can't disagree with that. But there is no reason to expect that this will be given to us instantaneously and in such a powerful and extraordinary manner. There is no reason to think that we do not need to prepare our messages beforehand. We have no reason to expect the room in which we pray for boldness to be shaken or to expect some other supernatural occurrence in answer to prayer. These differences are all important.

The very fact that the account in Acts 4 describes what God did for His *apostles* makes it clear that what they experienced was

---

3   See my book *Preaching According to the Holy Spirit*. While special, extraordinary powers were given to them by the Spirit, that does not mean that these were acquired apart from the means (here prayer). Paul, as an apostle, also was granted these powers; but he requested that the Ephesians and the Colossians pray for the very things promised (Eph. 6:19-20; Col. 4:2-4). Thus, he also shows that, at least in part, God used ordinary means to fulfill His extraordinary promise.

something special, something apostolic, something that was in fulfillment of what Jesus promised to *them*—not something promised to *us*. If that which is out of the ordinary becomes ordinary, as Cymbala seems to suppose, then the extraordinary event loses its effectiveness in authenticating them as inspired bearers of God's Word.[4] Books like *Fresh Wind, Fresh Fire*, which treat the New Testament accounts of what God did for the apostles in a similar manner throughout, tend to trivialize apostleship.

Perhaps from this example you can see the sort of thing that I address in this book. But before we move on, let's consider another example. In this chapter we shall limit ourselves to Cymbala's book because it is convenient and offers examples of many of the problems that we shall deal with. Listen to this:

> Are you and I seeing the results that Peter saw? Are we bringing thousands of men and women to Christ the way he did? If not, we need to get back to his power source ... When we sincerely turn to God, we will find that his church always moves *forward*, not *backward*.[5]

Are you and I promised thousands of converts? Is the reason why we are not seeing such conversions because of our lack of sincerity and our failure to get back to our power source—the Holy Spirit? First, there is nowhere that such a promise of great numbers of converts is made to us today. It is true that Jesus said to His disciples, "... whoever believes in Me will himself do the works that I am doing; indeed, he will do greater works than these because I am going to the Father" (John 14:12). Jesus makes it clear that the works that His disciples would do would be "greater" in the sense of being *more extensive* and continuing over a longer period of time.[6] His ministry had been confined to Palestine and to a period of three and one-half years; they would traverse the then-known world, preaching for the rest of their lives. That much,

---

4   Cf. 2 Corinthians 12:12; Hebrews 2:3-4. Then, *nothing* is extraordinary.
5   *Op. cit.,* p. 97.
6   They were not greater in *nature*; raising the dead is about as great a work as can be done!

as I said, is clear. But is the promise to everyone? Is it to us today? Are we to expect Peter's results?[7]

Chapters 13 through 17 of John's gospel are unique. Once again, it is important to recognize that what Jesus says in those chapters, He is saying primarily to the men who would become His apostles—those that He would "send off" as His ambassadors to preach and do mighty works in His Name. They were the first church missionaries.[8] But, as we shall see, they were missionaries extraordinaire! He had gathered them together for a few last words around the Passover feast that He celebrated with them. In doing so, He gave them assurances that were for them alone. For instance, in John 14:26, Jesus' words are recorded: "But the Counselor, the Holy Spirit, Whom the Father will send in My Name, He is the One Who will teach you everything and remind you of everything that I told you." Now, it is certain that this was a divine word to the apostles to be, and to no one else. They would be preaching inspired messages and writing inspired Scripture; they would need to know two things to do so.

First, they would need to know what Jesus had said and done. They had been with Him; they had accompanied Him during the three and one-half years of His ministry. But as fallible men, they would forget much. Moreover, there was much they didn't

---

7   We who are called to be pastor-teachers (Ephesians 4:11-12) have our work spelled out by those two designations; we are to shepherd and teach. We are not primarily called to do evangelism; rather, the work to which we are called is to build up and care for the flock to whom we minister (Acts 20:28-32). Making thousands of converts seems to have been a response that was due to the many Jews at Jerusalem and elsewhere whom John the Baptist prepared for the coming of Jesus by repentance, and to the preaching of Jesus Himself. One thing is sure: Peter was reaping the results of Jesus' prayer on the cross when He prayed, "Father forgive them, for they don't know what they are doing." God was answering that prayer. Forgiveness came by faith in the message preached by Peter. People are never forgiven apart from believing the gospel. Jesus' prayer included the means—preaching. Bringing men and women to Christ is the task of the evangelist (in particular) and of all Christians (including pastor-teachers) in general (Ephesians 4:11; Acts 8:1-4).
8   The Greek *apostello*, meaning "to send off" [usually, as a representative of another], from which "apostle" comes, and the Latin *mitto*, meaning "to send off," from which "missionary" comes, are exact equivalents.

understand, as the gospels often point out. They might get things garbled. So, they needed help that was beyond their own human ability because they would be writing Scripture. The Spirit, Jesus said, would come to enable them to remember—infallibly—what had happened so that the message that they would preach, and the gospels that they would write, would be inerrant. Those words do not apply to us: we do not write Scripture.

Second, there were new truths that would be needed as they carried on their work. These included such matters as guidance about where to go, exactly what to say in difficult situations, how to found and organize the church, and what to do about problems that would arise in the course of these activities. That second need would also be met by the Holy Spirit: "He is the One Who will teach you everything." Here is the promise that they would have all that they would ever need through the inspired teaching of the Spirit.[9]

Throughout these intimate chapters of John's gospel, Jesus' numerous references to the coming of the Spirit upon the disciples are recorded. In connection with these references, again and again He is entitled "the Spirit of truth." That title designates the Spirit as the One Who would "guide" them "into all truth" (John 16:13). In that verse, Jesus said that the Spirit would not only talk about the past or about the present; He would also "tell" them "things to come." But, again, Jesus made that promise, as well as the former one, to the *apostles*—not to everyone. Jesus was talking to no one else. He spoke about no other ministry than the apostolic ministry. The Lord Jesus had "much to tell" His disciples, but they weren't "able to bear" it at that time. That's why, subsequently, Jesus engaged the apostles and the prophets (those New Testament writers and speakers to whom God through the apostles gave power to speak infallibly and to compose inerrant Scripture) in revelatory tasks (Ephesians 3:5).

Furthermore, all of this would "happen" to the apostles, Jesus said, so that when it did happen *they* might "believe" (John 14:29).

---

9   That also means that there would be no need for further revelation once the Spirit taught them *everything* that was necessary for them and for Christ's people to know (cf. John 14:26).

To spread out to all Christians the tasks and the results that were promised to the apostles (who were given extraordinary power to accomplish them) is not only poor exegesis, but it is also irresponsible.

One more example should suffice. Take note of this. Cymbala writes:

> The Holy Spirit spoke to one of our choir members … "You know what? I believe God just showed me that we should lift up Carol in prayer. Would you all join me?"[10]

And that isn't all: supposedly the devil speaks as well. Here is a record of what Satan is reported to have said to Carol, Jim Cymbala's wife:

> You might have a big choir, and you're making albums and doing outreaches at Radio City Music Hall and all the rest. Fine, you and your husband can go ahead to reach the world for Christ—but I'm going to have your children. I've already got the first one. I'm coming for the next two.[11]

There you have it—continuing divine revelation to a choir member (and others mentioned in the book) and demonic revelation to the pastor's wife! I am not going to discuss these claims at this point beyond observing that, as we have just seen, all truth would be given to the apostles (John 16:13) when the Spirit came upon them. There would then be no need for special, individual revelation by the Spirit thereafter. Either all that would be needed was given to them, or it was not. We shall see later on how this promise was fulfilled during the apostolic age and how revelation ceased with the end of that era after the Scriptures were completed. For now, simply remember, the apostles were given all the truth they (or we) would ever need.[12]

So, there are two distinctly different ways of viewing the New Testament record. There is the way of Jim Cymbala and many

---

10   *Ibid.,* p. 103.
11   *Ibid.,* pp. 60, 61.
12   How was the choir member to know apart from a direct revelation given to her that Carol needed prayer? By the way in which the Scriptures tell us. We are to be so close to one another that we request and receive prayer from one another. Certainly there was no need for additional divine revelation in the matter.

charismatics: everything that we see happening to and through the apostles also should be happening in today's church. Then, there is the belief of the historic reformation churches: the special gifts of the Spirit were given to the apostles alone for special purposes during the apostolic era and ceased thereafter, their purpose and function having been fulfilled.[13] The book that you hold in your hands obviously espouses the latter view.

Now, just one more word. Throughout his book, Cymbala claims that today's church is impotent because it fails to draw upon the Spirit in apostolic ways. It has acquired a fossilized, Laodicean spirit. According to Cymbala, it is time for the fresh wind of the Spirit to blow across her dry bones and revive the church again. His solution? Prayer, prayer, and more prayer. Prayer is so emphasized that it takes on the character of a meritorious ritual. People pray around the clock, seven days a week! How many pray and how long they pray seems of great importance to Cymbala. Yet, Jesus spoke disparagingly of the heathen idea that they will be heard for their much speaking. He also condemned the Pharisees' long prayers as hypocritical. And James speaks of the "effectual, fervent prayer" of *one* man—Elijah—whose prayer accomplished "much." It is dangerous to substitute some ritualistic practice for sensible prayer and action according to the clear and balanced teaching of Scripture—the sort about which Jesus spoke in the Sermon on the Mount.

Is the church in trouble today? Yes. It's hard to deny that. Is there too great a dependence on human effort and not enough dependence on the Spirit and the Word? Yes. Well then, are the

---

13   Calvin wrote, "of the offices which Paul makes mention of, some are perpetual, others temporary ... those that are temporary, are such as were appointed at the beginning for the founding of the Church ... and these, in a short time afterwards, ceased" *Commentary: 1 Corinthians* 12:28. Elsewhere he said, "The gift of tongues, and other such like things, are ceased long ago in the Church" *Commentary: Acts* 10:44. And, he wrote, "For because Christ meant to set forth the beginning of His kingdom with those miracles, they lasted but for a time" *Commentary: Acts* 2:38. This view, expressed by the Reformation's most careful and respected theologian, reflected the common view among the Reformers. It has remained the standard Protestant interpretation of the phenomenon of the extraordinary gifts ever since.

many Cymbalas who are on the fringe of the church and who throw stones at her right? Absolutely not! Their diagnosis of the church's problems is shallow; it extends no further than to symptoms. They fail to reach the true causes.

CHAPTER 2

THE "LAST DAYS"

IN Acts 2:17-21, Peter quotes from Joel 2:
> *In the last days, God says,*
> *I will pour out My Spirit on all flesh,*
> *and your sons and your daughters will prophesy,*
> *your young men will see visions,*
> *and your old men will dream dreams;*
> *and even on My male and female slaves I will prophesy.*
> *I will perform wonders in the sky above*
> *and signs on the earth below—*
> *blood and fire and clouds of smoke.*
> *The sun will be darkened and the moon turned to blood*
> *before the great and glorious day of the Lord comes.*
> *Everybody who calls on the Lord's name will be saved.*

There should be no question about one thing: Peter is saying here that what Joel had predicted was being fulfilled in the Pentecostal event. But what occurred? According to Joel,

1. God poured out His Spirit;
2. This pouring took place in the "last days";
3. The pouring was upon "all flesh" (i.e., all sorts of people), such as sons, daughters, young men, old men, male and female servants of God.
4. They would see visions, dream dreams (presumably, both revelatory ones);
5. They would prophesy;
6. There would be upheavals of things that appeared to be permanent (like the heavenly bodies);
7. This would happen prior to the Lord's great, glorious day;

8. And whoever would call on the Name of the Lord would be saved.

Some things in this prophecy seem crystal clear. The Spirit would come. He did, as Peter tells us in unmistakable terms. This unique event included revelatory prophecy. All sorts of people—even those who had no special office—were able to perform wondrous works and become channels of special revelation as they saw visions, dreamed dreams from God, and prophesied. And this would take place "in the last days" or, as Joel puts it in verse 18, "in those days." Both of these references obviously refer to the same period. But it is important to notice that it was not merely the Pentecostal event that occurred in those days; the two expressions used in verses 17 and 18 that introduce the two parts of the prophecy (the first part about what would happen to the *people* involved, the second about the upheaval of seemingly permanent *fixtures* in the world) speak of what happened at Pentecost and in "the last *days*; those *days*." Don't miss the plural. Joel's prophecy about the pouring out of the Spirit was a significant part of the fulfillment of his words, but the passage clearly indicates that these miraculous, revelatory gifts and cosmic upheavals would occur *throughout* the "last days," *up until* the "great and glorious day of the Lord" (v. 20). Following that "day," the gifts would cease because the last days would have been brought to an end.

First, let's be clear about verses 19 through 20, which refer to the cosmic changes that were predicted. Did any such thing happen at Pentecost or during the apostolic period? Certainly not literally. Is this portion of the prophecy then yet to be fulfilled, as some think? No, there is no need to contradict Peter, who unmistakably declared that "this [what was happening then and there] is what the prophet Joel spoke about" (v. 16). What, then, do the cosmic changes refer to?

Throughout Old Testament prophecy, such descriptions are used figuratively to indicate the downfall and change of seemingly permanent political and social orders. See, for instance, the following:

The sun and moon grow dark
And the stars lose their brightness.   (Joel 3:15)

Behold, the day of the LORD is coming,
Cruel, with fury and burning anger,
To make the land a desolation;
And He will exterminate its sinners from it.
¹⁰ For the stars of heaven and their constellations
Will not flash forth their light;
The sun will be dark when it rises
And the moon will not shed its light.   (Isa. 13:9-10)

And all the host of heaven will wear away,
And the sky will be rolled up like a scroll;
All their hosts will also wither away
As a leaf withers from the vine,
Or as one withers from the fig tree.   (Isa. 34:4)

Near is the great day of the LORD,
Near and coming very quickly;
Listen, the day of the LORD!
In it the warrior cries out bitterly.
A day of wrath is that day,
A day of trouble and distress,
A day of destruction and desolation,
A day of darkness and gloom,
A day of clouds and thick darkness,
A day of trumpet and battle cry
Against the fortified cities
And the high corner towers.   (Zeph. 1:14–16)

"For behold, the day is coming, burning like a furnace; and all the
arrogant and every evildoer will be chaff; and the day that is coming
will set them ablaze," says the LORD of hosts, "so that it will leave
them neither root nor branch....
Behold, I am going to send you Elijah the prophet before the coming
of the great and terrible day of the LORD."   (Mal. 4:1, 5)

These prophecies each speak of some day of Yahweh that brings about massive changes in the destinies of seemingly unchangeable nations like Babylon. For Babylon to fall, we might say, is like the stars falling, the moon turned to blood, the sun failing to shine. That's how great, unexpected, and unthinkable the change that God brings about in a day of judgment.

In these last days, God was once again bringing judgment—this time on Israel. The many tongues with which the Spirit-endowed preachers on Pentecost spoke were indicative of the fact that physical Israel would no longer be able to lay an exclusive claim to the title "God's people." There would be a new spiritual nation, a new Israel, created out of all those who would trust in Jesus Christ (cf. 1 Peter 2:9, 10). The vineyard would be taken away from the former vine dressers who slew the Owner's Son, and given to others who would serve Him. The old order of Judaism was about to pass away. The temple would be destroyed, and the city would be leveled. There would be no more physical worship, because those who engaged in it had forgotten what its spiritual intent was to be. Instead, those who would worship God in Spirit and in truth from all the nations of the earth would be sought and found by God (John 4:24). The promise to Abraham, that in his seed all the nations of the earth would be blessed, was coming to pass. Some from every tribe and tongue and nation would come into the kingdom of God, which John and Jesus announced was "at hand," and which the apostles were now to go forth proclaiming. The prophecy of Daniel, that in the "time of the end" (Daniel 12:4) the Lord Jesus would approach the Ancient of Days in clouds to receive a kingdom that would never end and that, therefore, would never be given to another, at long last was being fulfilled (Daniel 7:13-14, 27).[1] That at the ascension Jesus was crowned "Lord" is explicitly revealed by Peter (Acts 2:36).

---

1   See Jay Adams and Milton Fisher, *The Time of the End: Daniel's Prophecy Reclaimed*, for details. In Hebrews 9:26 we are told that Jesus appeared "at the end of the ages." That is, the end of those ages up until His coming. See also Jude 17-18; 1 John 2:18; 1 Peter 4:7; James 5:5-9; Hebrews 1:2; 10:25 and Titus 2:12-13.

So, the "last days" was the time when all of this occurred. These days were the beginning of a period of revelatory and miraculous events. Does this mean that the last days extended throughout the entire New Testament era? Certainly not. The last days (or end of days) were the last days of the *Old Testament* era, the last days of the era in which Joel and Peter were living. It is quite wrong, therefore, to extend these days into our time, since those "last days," together with the events that were to transpire during them, were completed long ago. They constitute the forty-year period of grace given to Israel up until the final judgment in 70 AD. The "last days" were an overlapping period. The Old Testament era was officially closed, and the New Testament era had begun, but during that period of transition, as the one was petering out, the other was swiftly taking its place. By 70 AD the transition had been completed.

Many transitional factors are significant as we consider that period. It was an extraordinary time. It was what we might call the "apostolic age," the time when the apostles carried the gospel to the then-known world (cf. Acts 1:8; Colossians 1:23, 28). It was a time when God raised up prophets in His church who revealed God's Word to congregations in lieu of a completed written revelation. It was a time when, to authenticate their ministry, the apostles (like their Lord) performed authenticating miracles (cf. Acts 2:43; 2 Corinthians 12:12; Hebrews 2:1-4). It was a time when Jews and Christians alike frequented the temple and even participated in some of its ceremonies. It was a time when the issue of Gentile participation in the church, and particularly the issue of circumcision, was raised and settled at the Jerusalem conference (Acts 15). During "those days," the Spirit, Who was to assist the apostles and those who worked with them, wrought miracles through them, fell on persons at the Gentile "Pentecost" (Acts 10), and was given by the laying on of hands in Samaria and in Ephesus (the two spillovers from the greater Pentecosts on which Peter preached using the "keys" Jesus gave him to unlock the door to His church first admitting Jews, then Gentiles). What a period of hectic activity! What a period of change and unique and unusual events, events to be repeated in later periods that followed the "last days" of the Old Testament era. Remember, the "last days" extended only until the coming of the great and glorious day of the Lord (Acts 2:20). That day was the day of judgment in 70 AD.

From Joel's Old Testament perspective, this day of the Lord was the terminus of the last days of *his* age. From our perspective, it was not only that, but it was also the beginning of the new days of the kingdom of God in *our* era.

Jesus spoke of those last days as well; in His discourse on the Destruction of Jerusalem, He said:

> *But in those days, after that affliction,* **The sun will grow dark, and the moon will not give her light; the stars will fall from the sky**, *and the powers in the heavens will be shaken. At that time they will see* **the Son of Man coming in clouds** *with great power and glory. And at that time He will send out His angels, and they will gather together His chosen ones from the four winds, from the end of the earth to the end of the sky.*
>
> *Now learn a parable from the fig tree: Whenever its branch has already become tender and shoots forth leaves, you know that summer is near. So also with you—when you see these things happening, know that He is near, at the door. Let Me assure you that this generation surely will not pass away until all these things take place. Heaven and earth will pass away, but My words won't pass away. But about that date or hour—nobody knows it; not the angels in heaven, or the Son. Only the Father does. Watch out. Be alert because you don't know when that time will be. It's like a man leaving his house on a trip, who puts his slaves in charge of things, each with his task, and orders the doorkeeper to watch. So then, you must watch—because you don't know when the owner of the house will come, whether it will be in the evening, or at midnight, or when the rooster crows, or in the morning—so that if He comes suddenly He won't find you sleeping! Now what I say to you, I say to all—watch!*
>
> (Mk. 13:24-37)

Right after the affliction of those days, **The sun will grow dark and the moon will not give her light; the stars will fall** *from the sky and the powers of the heavens will be shaken. At that time the sign of the Son of Man will appear in heaven, and at that time all the tribes of the land will mourn, and they will see the* **Son of Man coming on the clouds of heaven** *with power and much glory. He will send out His messengers with* **a loud blast of the trumpet, and they will gather** *His chosen ones from the four winds, from one end of the heavens to the other.*

Now, learn a parable from the fig tree: when its branch becomes tender and shoots forth leaves, you know that summer is near. So too, when you see all of these things, know that He is near, at the door. Let Me assure you that this generation surely will not pass away until all these things take place.

(Mt. 24:29-34)

Now when you see Jerusalem surrounded by armies, then you know that its desolation has drawn near. At that time those who are in Judea must flee to the mountains, those who are in the city must leave and those who are in the country must not enter the city, because these are the days of vengeance, in which everything that is written will be fulfilled. Woe to pregnant women and to those who are nursing babies in those days! There is going to be great distress upon the land and wrath for this people. They will be cut down by the edge of the sword and will be led as captives into all sorts of lands, and Jerusalem will be trodden down by the Gentiles until the times of the Gentiles are fulfilled. There will be signs in the sun, the moon and the stars, and on the land nations will be tense and in perplexity at the roaring of the sea and the waves. People will collapse from fear and foreboding of what is coming upon the world, because the powers of the heavens will be shaken. Then at that time they will see the Son of Man coming on a cloud with power and great glory. So when these things begin to happen, straighten yourselves and raise your heads, because your redemption is drawing near.

> *Then He told them a parable:* **Look at the fig tree and all the**
> **trees.** *When they put forth leaves you can see and know yourselves*
> *that summer is already near. So too, when you see these things hap-*
> *pening, you can know that God's empire is near. Truly I tell you that*
> *this generation won't pass away until all this happens.*
> (Lk. 21:20-32)

In all of these passages it is plain that Jesus is speaking about the same period that Joel described. How do we know this? We know it because He says that there would be some disciples alive to see the destruction of Jerusalem (and the events leading up to it), which was the climax of the whole complex of last day events. They would be persecuted during that time, but they would be given the ability to best their persecutors in debate by the special power of the Holy Spirit (Luke 21:14-15).

In these passages we also read of the Lord Jesus coming in power on clouds of glory. This is the fulfillment of the Daniel 7 passage mentioned above. He was given the rule of the fifth kingdom in the days of Rome (the fourth kingdom of Daniel's vision) and "came" in visitation upon apostate Israel, which had rejected and put Him to death (Luke 21:22; Matthew 23:32; 34-36). The temple ("house") had been left desolate (Matthew 24:38). He had abandoned it to the abomination that made it desolate. It was to be destroyed by the idolatrous Roman forces under Titus.

So Pentecost was the beginning of the last days. The destruction of the city and the temple in 70 AD was the conclusion of the last days, the deadline when *all* that was prophesied about them would be fulfilled (Matthew 23:36; 24:33-34; Mark 13:30; Luke 21:22, 32). In each of these verses referring to the last days that lead up to and include the destruction of Jerusalem, the Lord assures us that *all* (a key term in each verse cited) would take place in that (His) generation. In other words, when the last times ended, all that God determined to do during those days had been accomplished.

One of the problems with the sort of exegesis that Cymbala and others do is that they fail to reckon with the peculiar nature of this unique period called the "last days." They assume that it was merely the beginning of the period in which we live. But they fail to see that it was also the *end* of the *previous* period which overlapped it. That it was a time of great change, confusion for many, great evangelistic effort such as the world had never seen and would never see again since the apostles are gone, entirely escapes them. They settle for a simplistic view of complex things. They say, "Well, those special gifts were in evidence then; why shouldn't they be a part of the church today?" And so they attempt to work them up in one way or another. They fail to see that because revelation was incomplete during this apostolic age, God temporarily placed prophets in His church who revealed His will to them. That is the concern of the next chapter.

CHAPTER 3

THE PARTIAL AND THE COMPLETE

THE widespread idea that 1 Corinthians 13:12 refers to the eternal state has probably come about as a result of the way several hymns interpret the verse. But these hymns—fine as they may be in other respects—have led us astray. Let's look at that verse, along with the context in which it is found:

> *Love never fails. If there are prophecies, they will be set aside; if there are languages, they will cease; if there is knowledge, it will be set aside. We know in part and we prophesy in part, but when that which is complete comes, that which is partial will be set aside. When I was a child I spoke like a child, I thought like a child, I reasoned like a child; but now that I have become a man I have set aside childish ways. Now we see dimly as if looking in a bronze mirror, then face to face; now I know partially, but then I shall know fully just as I am fully known. Now these three things continue: faith, hope, love; and the greatest of these is love.*
>
> (1 Cor. 13:8-13)

The words "face to face" and the words "then I shall know fully, just as I am fully known" are the ones that are particularly confusing. In the larger context (chapters 12-14), Paul has been discussing the Corinthians' unloving use of the spiritual gifts that by means of his apostolic powers he had given to them (1 Corinthians 1:4-7). He makes the point that these gifts were for the benefit of all, not for one's own benefit alone. Moreover, he is concerned that they should be used properly, not in some selfish and disorderly manner in church meetings. The Corinthians seem to have been enamored with the more showy gifts, such as the ability to speak in foreign languages (tongues) without having first studied them. He reminds them of the purpose for which tongues were given: to preach God's message to unbelievers—an evangelistic purpose (1 Corinthians 14:22). What was wrong was that some were using this gift in church meetings to show off. The gift of tongues, however, was not intended for use among believers. Evangelism was not to be the emphasis among believers when they came together.[1] Rather, as Paul said, everything was to be done for the purpose of *edification*[2] (1 Corinthians 14:26). Foreign languages could not edify unless they were interpreted. Edification involves mental processes that lead to understanding (1 Corinthians 14:1-19). Therefore, they were not to be used in church meetings apart from interpretation.[3] Prophecy, on the other hand, was profitable because it could be understood and therefore could edify. In his contrast of the two gifts in chapter 14, Paul clearly comes out on the side of prophecy as the more useful gift.

It seems that direct revelation from God was conveyed by both tongues and prophecy.[4] They would both be equally profitable to the body of believers for purposes of edification (building up) if tongues were interpreted. But why were these churches receiving special revelation from God while we do not today? That is a very important question. And the answer is found in the passage from 1 Corinthians 13 quoted above.

Notice several things:

1. Paul says that both tongues and prophecy (as well as the special gift of knowledge) were temporary: "Love never

---

1   Though, doubtless, the gospel was always made known; 1 Corinthians 14:23-25 indicates that an unbeliever would hear a message that could lead to his conversion.

2   That is, for the building up of the saints in their most holy faith. Cymbala, on the other hand, seems to make the regular meetings of the church primarily evangelistic.

3   Interpreted, they would take on the character of prophecy.

4   It is not clear what the "knowledge" mentioned in these passages refers to. It may have been some sort of ability to discern or understand circumstances (insight). At any rate, like tongues and prophecy, it too was a temporary, extraordinary gift of the Spirit.

fails. If there are prophecies, they will be set aside; if there are languages, they will cease; if there is knowledge, it will be set aside" (v. 8).

2. Prophecies would be "set aside." By whom? Presumably, by the One Who gave them—God. The word *katargeo* used here means "to set aside by annulling, abolishing." Clearly, as the language indicates, some outside force would be active in doing so. Practices do not set aside, abolish, or annul *themselves*. So it is evident that a time would come when God would step in to end the practice; He would give no more special revelation.

3. The gift of speaking in foreign languages without studying them would "cease." That is to say, they would either be caused to cease or they would simply peter out. Probably the latter is meant since the word *pauo* ("cease") is used instead of *katargeo*. However the change of verbs may be merely stylistic.[5] Either way, Paul said that tongues would not continue indefinitely.

4. The gift of knowledge—direct revelation of whatever sort— would likewise be "set aside" or annulled (*katargeo* once again is used).

5. In contrast to those three gifts, which Paul assures us will disappear from the scene at a certain time, faith, hope, and love would *continue*[6] (i.e., "remain;" the verb used here is *meno*, to "remain, continue, stay in place").

---

5   The writing in the chapter is poetic. If the meaning of *pauo* includes the idea of "petering out," it could not be used to describe an event occurring at Christ's second coming. According to Paul, that event (and those accompanying it) are instantaneous—"at the twinkling (flash) of an eye" (1_Cor. 15:52). The word, so understood, perfectly describes something that happened in the "last days." Since the apostles no longer conveyed the gift of tongues after 70 AD, as those persons who possessed the gift gradually died, the gift itself dribbled away.

6   These three qualities represent the *ordinary* works of the Spirit in the lives of all believers. In contrast to the *gifts* of the Spirit, they must be classified as the *fruit* of the Spirit (see Galatians 5).

So that is the setting in which the words that we are considering are found. Now, what does seeing "face to face" have to do with all of this? To what does "fully knowing just as we are fully known" refer?

In order to explain verse 8, in which the revelatory gifts are said to be temporary, Paul says that this is because the present revelation given through these gifts is only *partial* (v. 9: "We know *in part* and we prophesy *in part*"). He goes on to say that this partial revelation will be replaced by a full and complete one: "but when that which is complete comes, that which is partial will be set aside"[7] (v. 10). In other words, at that time there would be no need for further revelation since Christians would have all that they would ever need.

Now to drive home his point, Paul uses two illustrations (v. 11-12) of how the greater replaces the lesser. When he was a child he engaged in childish ways; when he became an adult, he put these ways aside in favor of adult ways. The temporary, partial revelation was like the childish ways that would be replaced by adult ones (the complete revelation).

The second example—the one that causes the confusion—is of a bronze mirror which, unlike our modern mirrors, reflected only an indistinct, or partial image (one sees in it "dimly"). Revelation, which was given by means that were temporary, was given in little bits and pieces. But when the complete revelation would take its place, it would be like seeing face to face, like knowing as fully as one is known when he is seen with the eye by *another*, rather than when he sees *himself* in a mirror. The indistinctness would be replaced by sharpness; that is to say, partial knowledge would be replaced by that which is complete ("full").

There is nothing about heaven, eternity, or the second coming here. The discussion is solely about revelation. It is partial revelation given by God through prophecy, properly interpreted tongues, and

---

7   The direct contrast between partial and complete ("perfect" in the KJV) shows that a complete revelation is what he has in mind. Plainly, in contrasting that which is partial or complete Paul is comparing apples and apples, not apples and oranges.

special knowledge that is the subject of Paul's discussion. He isn't introducing another subject here. Paul's illustration was mistaken by some hymn writers for something that it was never intended to be.

Can this be confirmed beyond a doubt? Certainly. Consider verse 13: "And now these things continue (*meno,* "remain"): faith, hope, and love; and the greatest of these is love." One can understand, if the words of verse 12 refer to the second coming or to heaven, that faith and love would remain—but what of hope? Why would hope remain? It would be replaced by the reality for which the believer hopes, would it not? Remember Paul's discussion of hope in Romans 8:20-25? There he speaks of the hope of the future redemption of the body and of the creation itself. And at the conclusion of that discussion he says, "But when you see what you hope for, that isn't hope. Who hopes for what he sees? (v. 24[b]). That, of course, is the question to ask if the second coming and the eternal state are in view. And the answer to that question that any sensible person would give must be the same as the answer assumed in Romans 8—"No one hopes for what he sees!"

Clearly, if verse 12 refers to *seeing some day in heaven as one is now seen from there*, verse 13 makes no sense. There would be no need to anticipate (the biblical meaning of hope) what he already is experiencing. It is plainly wrong, then, to say that verse 12 refers to seeing in heaven. It is seeing *directly*, rather than *indirectly* in a mirror, seeing clearly and *fully* as another sees you, rather than as you see yourself *partially* and dimly in a mirror, about which Paul was writing. When it came, the complete revelation would be like seeing clearly and fully, in contrast to the revelation through special gifts of the Spirit given dimly in bits and pieces at different places up to and during the time of Paul's writing. Because it would be so much better, completed revelation would replace partial revelation. The partial would be done away with or would fade away.

Here, then, is an important piece of information given to us by the great apostle who himself was involved in the process of producing the written revelation which shortly would be completed. The

Lord had informed the apostles,[8] as we see here, about the perfect (better translated "complete") revelation to come. This revelation was, of course, the Scriptures which we have in their completed form today. But at the time of Paul's writing, the Bible was incomplete. It was being put together during the apostolic age, the "last days" about which we have been speaking. This very letter to the Corinthians was a piece of the whole.

Though it is somewhat speculative, there is good reason to believe that all of the books of the New Testament were written before the destruction of Jerusalem in 70 AD. Interestingly, in a recent book, *Redating the New Testament*, liberal theologian John A. T. Robinson has strongly maintained the view that all the books were composed prior to 70 AD.[9] He factually points out that the destruction of Jerusalem "is never once mentioned as a past fact," and maintains that "the silence is as significant as the silence for Sherlock Holmes of the dog that did not bark."[10]

There are, of course, many other reasons for believing that the completion of the New Testament was achieved by 70 AD. Since the Spirit would guide the apostles into "all truth" (John 16:13) and would teach and remind the apostles of everything that Christ told them (John 14:26), we know that this written revelation was complete before the death of the apostles. Most, if not all of them, died prior to the destruction of Jerusalem.[11] They, and those who wrote under their direction, were the ones to whom these promises were given; They were not given to anyone else. We know that the synoptic gospels were written before the destruction of Jerusalem since they record Jesus' prediction of the event, but say nothing of

---

8   Possibly He did so during the forty days after the resurrection when He spoke about many things that would pertain to the kingdom (Acts 1:3). Since Paul was not present during these sessions, the Lord might have informed him of the matter by special revelation, or he may have learned about it from the other disciples.
9   J. A. T. Robinson (London: SCM Press, 1976).
10   *Op. cit.,* p.13.
11   Robinson even challenges the late dates attributed to the writings of the apostle John and makes a case for his early demise.

the fulfillment of the prediction. Peter and Paul[12] are said by Eusebius to have died in the Neronian persecution, immediately prior to 70 AD. The book of Hebrews has the temple still standing, with priests offering sacrifices daily. Revelation also speaks of the temple intact, and all of the internal evidence clearly refers to a time before the destruction of Jerusalem.[13] And so it goes. Indeed, as Robinson shows, there is no reason for not supposing that every book of the New Testament could have been written before the destruction of Jerusalem. It is not possible at this time to prove conclusively that they were. However, Robinson has persuasively demonstrated that there is no solid objection to the thesis so far as either the external or internal evidence is concerned.

In addition, there is one important piece of evidence coming from Clement of Alexandria that, if accurate, would certainly lead us to believe that the apostolic revelation ceased a year or two before 70 AD. If it is accurate, then "that [revelation] which is complete" would have been written and possessed by most or all of the congregations by that time. Clement says that

> the teaching of our Lord at His advent, beginning with Augustus and Tiberius, was completed in the middle of the times of Tiberius. And that of the apostles, embracing the ministry of Paul, ends with Nero.[14]

If Clement is correct—and there is no reason to doubt him—then all of the teaching of the apostles by word and by pen was completed before the Destruction occurred.

Since in God's providence the destruction of the city of Jerusalem and the temple was the culmination for the transitional apostolic period, when the final end of the old system would come about, there are both good theoretical and doctrinal reasons for accepting Clement's position. There could be no more worship in the city. The

---

12   Robinson dates the latest of Paul's epistles (II Timothy) at autumn, 58 AD. *Ibid.*, p. 84.
13   I have discussed the internal evidence for this in my book, *The Time is at Hand*.
14   In R. C. Sproul, *The Last Days of Jesus* (Grand Rapids: Baker Books, 1999), p.144.

church at last was thoroughly separated from the temple and the synagog. The old system, which until 70 AD was struggling to stay alive, was now given its death blow. The apostles had carried the gospel to the then-known world in fulfillment of their commission (cf. Colossians 1:23, 28).[1] There was no more for them to do. Their ministries were over. God took them to be with Himself. It makes a neat package.

I will grant you that there is some conjecture about when exactly the revelation was complete, but there is no guesswork to be done about the meaning of 1 Corinthians 13. The complete revelation would replace the partial one. That final revelation would be for all of the churches. It would be in written rather than spoken form. It would be the standard by which the whole church would be governed for all of its existence. That much is clear. And, according to chapters 13 through 17 in John's Gospel, it was to the apostles that the Spirit of truth[2] would be sent to help them remember what Jesus had done and said, and to guide them into all new truth—that would consist of everything that they (or we) would ever need. That much is certain.

One more thing remains to be noted. In John 15:15, Jesus tells His disciples that He has made known to them "everything" that He has heard from His Father. That is to say, all the truth that they would ever need, that which the Father thought necessary for them to know, had been taught to them by the Lord Jesus Himself. And when the Spirit would come upon them, Jesus said He would help them to remember all of those teachings. When He says that the Counselor would speak about Him (John 15:26) and "His things" (John 16:14), that is doubtless what Jesus referred to.

I would like to close this chapter with the pointed words of John Calvin:

---

1   Calvin wrote: "Now the ascension of Christ was soon afterwards followed by a wonderful conversion of the world, in which the divinity of Christ was more powerfully displayed than while he dwelt among men." *Commentary*: John 14:12.
2   He is the teacher of truth (see 1 John 2:20).

That very *Spirit* had *led them into all truth,* when they committed to writing the substance of their doctrine. Whoever imagines that anything must be added to their doctrine, as if it were imperfect and but half-finished, not only accuses the apostles of dishonesty, but blasphemes against the *Spirit.*[3]

In short, the Cymbalas in the church, who want to arrogate to themselves what Christ gave only to the apostles, need to take heed.

---

3   *Commentary* on John 16:12 (italics his).

CHAPTER 4
INTERPRETING PROPERLY

IMMEDIATELY the objection arises, "Well, if John 13 through 17 was for the apostles, and much of what we read about in the Acts of the Apostles concerning the supernatural occurrences recorded there as well as a great deal that is referred to in the epistles (for example, the passages in I Corinthians that we have been considering) are not directly applicable to us, of what use is this material?" In addition, the objection might be raised, "How do we separate out what is applicable from what is not?" These are important questions that ought to be asked—and that need to be answered.

First, recognize that a great deal of what the Lord Jesus did that is recorded in the Bible is of a similar nature. His miracles, many of His actions, and much that He said have no direct application to us. For instance, we are not to imitate His example of riding into Jerusalem on a donkey. We are not to die for the sins of others. We cannot declare that we are the Bread of Life. Yet these facts cause us no difficulty.

Take much that is found in the Old Testament narratives as further examples of this. We cannot make the sun stand still, we have nothing to do with the physical ark of the covenant or the temple, and we do not predict the future exile of God's people to Babylon.

How, then, do we handle passages where we find such things? Are we simply to read and learn—or, perhaps, read and yearn? Certainly not! All of these passages are for our benefit. Listen to the words of the apostle Paul:

> I don't want you to be ignorant, brothers, about our fathers. They were all under the cloud, and all passed through the sea, and all were baptized into Moses in the cloud and in the sea, and all ate the same

spiritual food, and all drank the same spiritual drink; they drank from the spiritual Rock that followed (and the Rock was Christ). But with most of them God was displeased, and their bodies were scattered over the desert.

Now these events happened as examples for us so that we might not desire evil things as they did. Don't become idolaters as some of them were; as it is written: **The people sat down to eat and drink and stood up to revel**. *We must not commit sexual sins as some of them did, and twenty-three thousand fell in a single day. Neither should we test the Lord as some of them did and were destroyed by snakes. Nor grumble as some of them did and were destroyed by the destroyer. Now these events happened to them as examples and were recorded as counsel for us who live at this late date in history. So then, let the one who thinks that he stands watch out lest he fall. No trial has taken hold of you except that which other people have experienced; but God is faithful Who will not allow you to be tried beyond what you are able to bear, but rather, will provide together with the trial the way out so that you may be able to endure it.*

(1 Cor. 10:1-13)

You see, the recording of the events of God's dealings with His people, though they took place in different times and situations, are nevertheless applicable to us. At the very least they have an exemplary function (vv. 6, 11). While conditions are not precisely parallel to those that existed in the wilderness, for instance, there are parallels that make the record of Israel's sin and God's response to it valuable for us today. The people of Israel became involved in idolatry; we may also do so (hence, v. 7). Our idolatry may not involve a golden calf, but it may readily involve a lust for gold itself. This rebellious idolatry happened, Paul says, because the people desired evil things (v. 6). We, too, must be careful about allowing our desires to control us. When we become part of wild excesses in which we drink and revel, we too may find ourselves committing sexual sins (vv. 7-8). And so on.

Plainly, like the apostle Paul, who applied it to the church at Corinth, we may find teaching in such passages of the Old Testament that pertains to our lives. But to do so, we must "translate" that teaching out of the situation in which it was given into our present situation. That means looking for the principles at work in the passage that do apply to us.

Listen again to the apostle Paul:

> *Whatever was written before was written for our instruction, that by the endurance and the encouragement that the Scriptures give us we may have hope.*
>
> *(Romans 15:4)*

Notice that the biblical record has a purpose. As we saw previously, Paul once again says that the recording of events and sayings in the Scriptures was "for our instruction." We must never get away from that fact. Everything in the Bible has value for us. But it cannot all be applied *directly* to us in some one-to-one correspondence. As Paul says here in Romans, we must look for those things that will encourage us to endure. As he did in 1 Corinthians 10, we must take to heart those warnings and examples that reveal human weakness and sin, and learn from them. Yet that does not mean that we will be tempted with a golden calf, by manna that becomes boring, or by the same revels that tempted them to commit adultery. Rather, the temptation may come in the form of a new car, a larger house that we cannot afford, a job that we are getting tired of, or a flirtatious secretary. It is the *principles* involved that are significant, not the exact circumstances. As sinners, we do desire evil things; we do complain about our circumstances; we are tempted to sin sexually. Those are the constants, not secondary factors such as whether we are living in a day of miracles or not. These constants are relevant to God's people in all times. Where there are *some* correspondences and *some* elements of similarity to which the principle or truth applies, we are entitled—indeed, required—to make the application accordingly.

How can we gain encouragement to endure from the Scriptures, as Paul indicates we should in Romans 15:4? Not by thinking that, like an apostle, we will find the doors of our prison cell spring open when an angel appears to free us. That is not what we should expect. That was the *special* work of God by which He was authenticating His *special* message and His *special* messenger delivering it. But we should take heart in seeing that God did not forget or forsake his suffering servant who was undergoing trial for Christ's sake. The principle? That God cares for the faithful in difficult circumstances. *How* He will care for us may differ radically—even as it did in biblical times.[4] It may not be by delivering us from fiery furnaces or from lions' dens; however, He may deliver us from the machinations of a wicked boss or a devilish relative in some less spectacular way. Just because the miracle took place in the past is no reason to expect that it will do so again. Indeed, all we have been learning so far indicates that we may be certain that the time of the miraculous is over: we no longer live in a period of Old Testament or New Testament revelation. The revelation is complete. That which authenticates it is no longer needed (but, on this, see the next chapter).

We tend to think of that which is spectacular as more important than that which is not. That was, in part, the Corinthians' mistake. However, as we saw in Paul's comparison of prophecy and speaking in tongues, often the opposite is true.[5] Indeed, it is the normal, peaceful existence—apart from the spectacular one—that the Scriptures commend to us. Paul wrote to the Thessalonians: "eagerly aspire to live a quiet life" (1 Thessalonians 4:11; see also Romans 12:18). That is the sort of lifestyle that we must seek to live. The dramatic life, punctuated by crises and miracles, as described in Cymbala's book, must not be considered the Christian's norm. Times of trial, turmoil, and persecution will come. Unusual happenings and remarkable providences from God will take place. But the normal Christian life tends to be one of *shalom*: peace of heart and of lifestyle.

---

4   Cf. the distinct ways of God with His faithful that are mentioned in Hebrews 11.
5   In 1 Corinthians 12:31 Paul orders the church to "desire the greater gifts," thereby ranking them on different levels.

How do we "translate" passages having to do with the miraculous so as to apply them to non-miraculous circumstances today? As we have been illustrating, we can remove the miraculous element from the story or statement, and work with whatever else remains. For instance, the miraculous in Christ's death on the cross, by which He gave his life as a ransom for many, cannot be an example for us. We cannot die to redeem anyone. Yet, in Philippians 2, Paul uses the *attitude* that led to the sacrificial death of Jesus as an example for us that will lead to unity in the church of Christ. He urges us to have the same "mind" (attitude) as Christ did. We are to have the same concern for others, one that focuses on their advantages rather than on our own. As Jesus put others before Himself, abandoning all for our sakes and enduring the cross, Paul says that we too must put others' interests before our own. Carefully read the passage to see how Paul "translates" it and applies it to the lives of Christians who needed to become united:

> So then, if there is any encouragement in Christ, if there is motivating power in love, if there is any fellowship that comes from the Spirit, if there are any feelings of affection and compassion, then make my joy complete by thinking alike, having mutual love, being united in soul, thinking as one. Do nothing out of selfishness or vanity, but rather in humility consider others better than yourselves. Each of you should not only look out for his own interests but also the interests of others.
>
> You must think about yourselves what Christ Jesus thought about Himself. He, while existing in the form of God, didn't consider His equality with God something to be graspingly held onto at all costs, but, instead he emptied Himself, taking the form of a slave, becoming like a human being. Being found in human appearance, He humbled Himself, becoming obedient even to the point of death—death by a cross! As a result, God highly exalted Him and gave to Him the name above all names, so that at this name that He gave Jesus **every knee** of heavenly beings and earthly beings and beings under the earth **should bend**, and every tongue should confess that Jesus Christ is LORD to the glory of God the Father. So then, my

> *dear friends, just as you have always obeyed before (not only when I*
> *am present, but even more so when I am absent), work out your own*
> *solution to the problem with fear and trembling, since it is God Who*
> *is producing in you both the willingness and the ability to do the*
> *things that please Him.*
>
> *(Philippians 2:1-13)*

Sometimes we are hesitant to make the translation—especially when it is a matter of learning how to live from the life and death of Christ. But the apostles seem to have no problem in doing this, as we see here by Paul's use of Christ's death in Philippians 2.

Peter does much the same thing. He also "translates" the cross of Christ into material applicable to us. Consider his words in 1 Peter 2:18-23:

> *Household servants, submit yourselves to your masters, showing full*
> *respect, not only to those who are good and lenient but also to those*
> *who are cruel. One finds favor if, out of conscience toward God, he*
> *bears up under pain when suffering unjustly. Indeed, what credit is*
> *coming to you if when you are beaten for sinning you endure it? But*
> *if you endure suffering for doing good, this finds favor with God. In*
> *fact, you were called to this, since Christ Himself suffered in your*
> *place, leaving behind a pattern for you to copy so that you might fol-*
> *low in His steps:* **He committed no sin, nor was deceit found in**
> **His mouth.** *When He was insulted, He returned no insults; when*
> *He suffered, He made no threats, but entrusted Himself to the One*
> *Who does judge righteously.*

In using the death of Jesus Christ as an example for us to follow in one way or another (Paul notes the attitude of putting others first, Peter stresses Jesus' lack of retaliation and His trust in His Father), the elements of the death that might be applicable to us are singled out, while those that are not are not so used. Clearly, the apostles found it possible to do such things and thereby set the course for us to do the same.[6]

---

6   I have focused on the use of the cross since it is one that might seem least appropriate to "translation."

Take another example of a "translated" scriptural passage so as to bring home to the reader the aspect of the passage applicable to us today: Paul's use of Deuteronomy 25:4. In 1 Corinthians 9:9-10 he says,

> It is written in Moses' law, **Don't muzzle an ox when it is threshing.** *It isn't about oxen that God is concerned, is it? Isn't He really speaking about us? It was written for us, because when the plowman plows, and the thresher threshes, he should do so in hope of having a share of the crop.*

Now, when Paul asks, "It isn't about oxen that God is concerned, is it?" he is helping the reader think through the process of "translating" into his own context a passage that applies in principle, but not in its original application, circumstance, or form. Wasn't God concerned about oxen? Yes. "But Paul implies that he wasn't," you say. True. But what he means is simply this: the principle that one should not muzzle the ox as he treads out the grain is much larger than the particular application to oxen found in the law. Indeed, it should be of importance to us to see the hermeneutical method that Paul uses here. It is instructive to know that whenever a principle that has a life of its own is encountered, we must not confine it to the particular application in the context where we encounter it. Here, Paul extracts the principle and applies it to the paying of Christian workers.[1]

Do you begin to understand, then, that if Paul can so treat a straightforward passage in the law in the fashion that he treated Deuteronomy 25:4, stripping it of its particulars so as to get at the kernel principle to find guidance concerning God's ways with men, we too may do the same with passages by laying aside the supernatural elements. We may find help and glean from passages in which miraculous elements appear for this non-revelatory, non-miraculous period in which we live. Strip the events in the Gospels or in the book of Acts of the temporary, miraculous elements, and look for

---

1   It is a bit of a stretch, I'll grant you, if I apply Deuteronomy 25:4 on Thanksgiving day while I am slicing (and eating) the turkey! Yet, the translation *process* involved is identical.

the permanent features that remain. It is those features that you must apply to life today.

Failing to recognize the New Testament way of translating Old Testament passages leads the charismatic astray. He does not do what Paul, the master exegete and interpreter of Scripture, does. He wants to have it all. He will not settle for a part. He will not focus on the translatable, applicable part, as Peter does when isolating Christ's meekness as a lamb led to slaughter. Consequently, he goes astray.

Back to Cymbala's book for a moment. In justifying the exorcism of demons, in which he engages, here is what he says: "I believe in confronting Satanic activity ... the kind of thing Jesus and the apostles did on a regular basis."[2] Notice the assumption behind the method: "Jesus and the apostles did so; why shouldn't I?" The answer is plain: Cymbala, and other charismatics, are neither Jesus nor apostles. They are not even in a league with the seventy who are mentioned in Luke 10. When Jesus sent them, He gave them a special commission and the requisite power to fulfill it. He said, "See, I have given you authority to step on snakes and scorpions, and over all the enemy's power; nothing at all shall hurt you. However, don't rejoice that the spirits submit to you; rather, rejoice that your names have been enrolled in the heavens" (Luke 10:19-20). Surely, that authority was limited to the number of persons mentioned (actually numbered!) and to the mission on which they were sent; the promises accompanying their commission are not for all Christians at all times! It is also questionable whether or not the seventy retained the powers they were granted after the mission was complete.

Then we hear such non-sequiturs as, "But you are limiting God." No, we are not limiting God. God has all the power that He has always had. He doesn't change. However, He does not always exhibit His power in the same ways in every era, in every circumstance, or through every person. God was silent for four hundred years during the inter-testamental period. There was no revelation, and there

---

2   *Op. cit.*, p. 111.

were no prophets from Malachi to John. Does that mean that God was limited? Absolutely not! God simply does some things in one era that He does not do in another. And even in one era, not every promise fits all. The charismatic tends to see no such differences, make no such distinctions; he thinks that unless the same-sized sock fits all, there is something wrong with the foot one is unsuccessfully attempting to dress.

Because you and I do not expect to raise the dead as Jesus and Paul did, that does not mean that God is thereby limited. It simply means that He has not commanded or empowered you to do so. It is not a part of your task in this world at this time. So to say that God is limited because there are no extraordinary gifts today is to beg the question. There are no such gifts manifest because God has chosen not to manifest them (in spite of the claims made and the exhibitions that accompany those claims). And He has told us why: the Bible is complete. But what has that to do with the cessation of miraculous gifts? In the next chapter we shall consider that matter.

CHAPTER 5

AUTHENTICITY IS CENTRAL

As we have seen, the matter of partial revelation lies at the heart of the issue of extraordinary gifts. Until the church possessed a complete, written revelation, each congregation needed a way of discovering the Lord's will. The revelatory gifts of prophecy, knowledge, and tongues provided the channel that was needed. These gifts were transmitted by the apostles through the laying on of hands: "And as Paul laid his hands on them, the Holy Spirit came upon them, and they spoke in different languages and prophesied" (Acts 19:6). Presumably, that's what Paul was referring to in 1 Corinthians 1:7 when he told the church that they "didn't lack in any gift." He was reassuring them that he had treated them in this regard as well as any other church. He had given them all the gifts that they needed.

But revelation—as important as it was—was not the sole object of the provision of extraordinary gifts. Clearly, a second and equally important factor was involved. That is *the authenticating factor*. The extraordinary gifts signaled that something unusual was going on; they called attention to and authenticated the messenger and his message.

This authenticating factor is clearly spelled out in the New Testament. Consider Acts 2:22. At the beginning of his Pentecostal message, the apostle Peter, who was speaking to a crowd that had been gathered together because of the authenticating power of the Spirit's gifts given to him, referred to Jesus as "a Man from God accredited to you by miracles and wonders and the signs that God performed in your midst …" Note several things:

1. Even Jesus needed the authenticating gifts to accredit Him before Israel.

2. It was God the Father Who performed the signs and wonders through Jesus.
3. Jesus' miracles were of the sort that could be either verified or debunked by those who saw them since they were done in their presence.
4. The works Jesus did are described as miracles, wonders, and signs.

The first three items just listed (in points 1-3) are plain enough and need no explanation. However, the three words, "miracles, wonders and signs," could use a bit of exposition. They do not describe three different kinds of works, but three aspects of the same works. The word translated "miracles" is, literally, "powers." It speaks of the nature of the work itself: a miracle is an extraordinarily powerful work, one that couldn't happen in the ordinary course of life's activities. For instance, it would take more than ordinary human power to heal the sick with a word, cast out a legion of demons, or raise the dead. "Powers" would call attention to the one performing them.

The second term, "wonders," describes the effect that the powerful work has upon those who observe it. They are caused to wonder. It creates a sensation by amazing those who see it, and it causes them to talk and think about what is happening.

The third word, "signs," indicates the purpose of the mighty work: it is a sign or signal to those who observe. To say that it has sign value means that it should cause observers to recognize that the miracle-worker has more than human ability and should be heard. He is marked out, separated from the crowd as "a man from God."

Now, on the day of Pentecost, Peter was able to say this about the Lord Jesus because God regularly did marvelous works by Him:

And He went all over Galilee, teaching in their synagogs, preaching the good news about the kingdom and curing every sort of disease and illness among the people. A report about Him went out to all of Syria, and they brought to Him all the sick who were suffering from various diseases and painful illnesses, demoniacs, epileptics, and para-

lytics, and He healed them. Large crowds from Galilee, the Decapolis,
Jerusalem, Judea, and from the Jordan followed Him.

(Matthew 4:23-25)

As you can see, the signs and wonders that Jesus did attracted
crowds from all over Palestine (v. 25). That, as Peter said, was one
of the purposes of the sign gifts.[3] Moreover, when John sent his disciples to Jesus asking whether He was the One to come or whether
there would be another, Jesus' reply was in terms of the miracles
that He had performed in fulfillment of prophecy:

But when John heard in prison about Christ's deeds, by his disciples
he sent and asked Him, "Are You the coming One or should we
expect someone different?" Jesus answered them by saying, "Go tell
*John what you hear and see—***blind men see again** *and lame people*
walk, lepers are cleansed and deaf persons hear, the dead are raised
and the **poor have the good news announced to them***. Whoever*
doesn't stumble over Me is happy."

(Matthew 11:2-6)

Obviously, Jesus used the Spirit-given power to perform miracles in order to identify Himself to John as the Messiah. So, clearly,
miracles served an authenticating function for Him.

But what of the apostles? Did miracles also identify them as men
from God? Indeed they did. As a matter of fact, one of the marks
of an apostle was his ability to perform miracles. Here is what the
apostle Paul had to say about the matter:

The signs of the true apostles were performed among you with great
patience, by signs and by wonders and by supernatural works.

(2 Corinthians 12:12)

The apostle Paul was quite sensitive to this issue since he had not
been among the original twelve, but was an apostle born out of time.
Some, therefore, questioned his calling as an apostle. Moreover, in
his second letter to the church at Corinth, he had to distinguish
himself from false apostles. One of those distinguishing factors, he

---

3   We must not forget the element of compassion involved in the acts of
mercy that accompanied these sign gifts. That, however, is aside from the point
that is being made in this chapter.

points out, was the fact that he had performed miracles in their midst. And over against the false teachers, who also claimed to be apostles, he could say that a *"true* apostle" was to be identified as such by these signs. They were the signs of an apostle. Wherever there were miracles, in one way or another, you could know that an apostle was associated with them.

One of the strange things about those who claim that all Christians ought to be working miracles (speaking in tongues, prophesying, etc.) is that they do not seem to understand the point that Paul made. They claim that their supposed sign gifts come directly from God, not through the hands of apostles, as we saw them given in Acts 19. But everyone did not receive the gifts directly. It was only at the opening of the door of the church to the Jews (Acts 2) and to the Gentiles (Acts 10)—two very special occasions—that the Spirit came directly, without mediation. Clearly, that happened to demonstrate that God was admitting believers of both sorts into His church. On those two unique occasions, Peter was using the keys that Jesus gave him,[4] preaching Christ to both Jew and Greek. However, later on, when the Spirit was given to the Samaritans and to the Ephesians [events that were spillovers from the two greater (we might even say "key") events mentioned above], gifts were conferred by the laying on of the apostles' hands.

> *Now when the apostles in Jerusalem heard that Samaria had accepted God's word, they sent Peter and John to them. They went down and prayed for them, so that they might receive the Holy Spirit (so far, He hadn't fallen on any of them; they had simply been baptized in the name of the Lord Jesus). Then they laid their hands on them and they received the Holy Spirit.   (Acts 8:14-17)*
>
> *While Apollos was in Corinth, Paul, traveling by the upper route, came to Ephesus. He found some disciples and said to them, "Did you receive the Holy Spirit when you believed?" They replied, "No, we haven't even heard that there is a Holy Spirit." So he said, "Into what, then, were you baptized?" They said, "Into John's baptism."*

---

4   Cf. Matthew 16:18-19.

Paul said, "John baptized with a baptism of repentance, telling the people to believe in the One coming after him—in Jesus." When they heard this, they were baptized into the name of the Lord Jesus. As Paul laid his hands on them, the Holy Spirit came upon them, and they spoke in different languages and prophesied.   (Acts 19:1-6)

So from that time on, gifts were only given indirectly by the apostles.

Suppose I say to you, "Our new church is meeting in a home on High Street. You can't miss it. There is a sign out front on the lawn." You are assured that it will be easy to identify the house because of the sign. However, when you arrive at the right block of High Street, every house is identical—even to the fact that each one has a similar sign. Under those conditions, the sign has no sign *value* (the ability to mark out something from among many in order to identify it). It serves no purpose if every house has one. So, too, if every Christian may possess special gifts directly (apart from apostolic donation), and not the apostles only, then these gifts can no longer be "signs of a true apostle." Either Paul was right or Paul was wrong in so speaking in 2 Corinthians 12:12.

Since the ability to perform wonders and to give this ability to others was a prerogative of the apostle, the gifts would cease with the death of the last apostle and of the last one to whom the apostles granted such gifts by the laying on of hands. There isn't one shred of evidence in the Bible that these gifts would persist beyond the apostolic age. The gifts were to identify the messengers who were to establish the church as true apostles ("missionaries") of the Lord Jesus Christ.

Not only did the signs and wonders identify a messenger from God, they also authenticated the message that he proclaimed:

If the word spoken through angels was certain, and every transgression and disobedience received its full punishment, how can we escape if we neglect such a great salvation? It was at the outset declared by the Lord, and it was confirmed to us by those who heard Him. God also testified to it by signs, wonders, all sorts of miracles and gifts from the Holy Spirit, distributed as He wished.

(Hebrews 2:2-4)

The writer of Hebrews says that the salvation message was first declared by the Lord Jesus Christ and afterwards was preached by the apostles who heard Him (v. 3). Then he says that God bore witness to the truth of what the Lord and His apostles preached. How? He "testified" to the message with signs, wonders, all kinds of miracles and gifts from the Holy Spirit. It is significant that he mentions not only the other miracles, but also the Spirit's "gifts." They were not to be separated from other miracles as if their purpose was other than to "witness" to the authenticity of the apostolic message. Their sign function was precisely the same.

So there is every reason to think that the sign gifts have ceased, since the apostles and those they laid their hands on to confer gifts of one sort or another are long gone. There is absolutely no reason to think otherwise. To maintain that we, in our time, are in exactly the same situation as the apostolic church is preposterous. Yet that is exactly what Cymbala, and others like him, maintain. If they are to establish their claims, they must show us that apostles still exist, that they are *true* apostles (evidenced by the signs and wonders that they perform), and (hearkening back to previous chapters) that there is a need for additional revelation today, which must be authenticated by these miracles. Such a task is impossible. God has made it so by the way in which He has framed the matter in His Word. He has left no room for doubt; His Word eliminates those claims which do not fit the biblical rubrics.

Now, while it is true that signs and wonders authenticated the true messenger and message of God, there were always those who purported to be prophets and miracle workers—who were not. Instead, they were false prophets. Jesus warned against such persons:

> In response, Jesus said to them, "Watch out that nobody misleads you. Many will come in My Name, saying, 'I am the Christ,' and they will mislead many ... and many false prophets will arise and will mislead many ... "

> (Matthew 24:4-5, 11).

Similarly, Paul warned the elders of the church at Ephesus:

I know that after my departure fierce wolves will enter in among you, not sparing the flock, and from among yourselves men will arise speaking distorted things to drag away disciples to follow them. Therefore, be alert, remembering that for three years, night and day, I didn't stop counseling each one of you with tears.

(Acts 20:29-31)

Therefore, today we ought to be aware of this fact and remain alert to the inroads of the evil one into the church through those who preach a false message and who attempt to support it by means of "lying powers and signs and wonders" (as Paul put it in 2 Thessalonians 2:9-10). He speaks of the many types of "unrighteous deceptions" that these persons practice (v. 10). If everyone who pretends to perform miracles is to be believed simply on that basis alone, we would all be duped in no time flat! Even the Mormons claim to do miracles.

"Well," you say, "if there are true and false miracles, how is one to distinguish between the two?" First, let it be clear, I have just established above that there is no longer any need to do so. The apostolic age is past. There are no more apostles who must be authenticated as "true" by means of miracles. There is no new revelation to be "confirmed" by signs and wonders. That which is "complete" has come. So the problem no longer exists. Every supposed instance of extraordinary gifts, by definition, constitutes a false claim. Either the person claiming them is a deceiver or is self-deceived. We have unquestionably established from the biblical record that there is no reason to expect miracles in our time.

But in the days of the apostles, as in previous periods of miracles, there had to be a test to distinguish the true claims from the false. What was it? It was twofold. In Deuteronomy 18:20-22, God addressed the subject:

But the prophet who speaks a word presumptuously in My name which I have not commanded him to speak, or which he speaks in the name of other gods, that prophet shall die. "You may say in your heart, 'How will we know the word which the LORD has not spoken?' " When a prophet speaks in the name of the LORD, if the thing does not come about or come true, that is the thing which the LORD has not spoken. The prophet has spoken it presumptuously; you shall not be afraid of him.

Obviously, if the prophecy fails, the prophet has failed. That is the first element in determining who is and who is not a false prophet. And, incidentally, if you want to discover how seriously God takes the matter of false prophecy, note that He considered it to be nothing short of a capital offense (v. 20). To lead God's people astray is no light matter in God's eyes. So it is important for us to take the matter seriously.

But there is more to be learned. In Deuteronomy 13:1-5, God set forth another crucial element by which to distinguish between a true or false prophet:

If a prophet or a dreamer of dreams arises among you and gives you a sign or a wonder, and the sign or the wonder comes true, concerning which he spoke to you, saying, "Let us go after other gods (whom you have not known) and let us serve them," you shall not listen to the words of that prophet or that dreamer of dreams; for the LORD your God is testing you to find out if you love the LORD your God with all your heart and with all your soul. You shall follow the LORD your God and fear Him; and you shall keep His commandments, listen to His voice, serve Him, and cling to Him. But that prophet or that dreamer of dreams shall be put to death, because he has counseled rebellion against the LORD your God who brought you from the land of Egypt and redeemed you from the house of slavery, to seduce you from the way in which the Lord your God commanded you to walk. So you shall purge the evil from among you.

In substance, what this is saying is that God often tests His people through false prophets. Have you ever thought of the matter that way before? He wants to see if they will remain steadfast to the truths they have learned. So, from time to time, when a false teacher comes along, says he will perform signs of one sort or another, and to all outward appearances does, the believer still must not follow him—and here's the crucial factor—*if his doctrine is defective* (vv.

2-3). One must not follow a teacher who teaches what is contrary to God's Word. Again, that dovetails today with the idea that there is no more revelation forthcoming; the Bible is the complete revelation. So, every teaching that does not conform to the Bible is the teaching of a false prophet.

Clearly, then, it is not merely signs that confirm. As Paul said, lying "signs" can deceive. The two elements must converge: there must be signs *plus* teaching that is true to the apostolic message. But the one is of greater importance than the other. According to Deuteronomy 13, the doctrinal matter overrides the experiential one (the supposed sign). It is the factor that helps distinguish true miracle working from, for instance, that of the Egyptian priests who opposed Moses.[1]

One more passage from the New Testament that confirms the importance of doctrine—even over signs—is found in 1 John 4:1-6:

Dear friends, don't believe every spirit, but test the spirits to discover whether they are of God, because many false prophets have gone out into the world. By this you know God's Spirit: every spirit that confesses that Jesus Christ has come in flesh is from God, and every spirit that doesn't confess Jesus isn't from God; indeed, this is the spirit of antichrist that you have heard is coming (and now is in the world already). Dear children, you are of God and have defeated them since the One Who is in you is greater than the one who is in the world. They are of the world; therefore, what they say is of the world and the world listens to them. We are of God; whoever knows God listens to us, but whoever isn't of God doesn't listen to us. From this we know the spirit of truth and the spirit of error.

Here, the spirits are to be tested in terms of what they teach.

---

1   If the supposed miracle looks genuine but the doctrine is in error, the miracle-worker must not be accepted. This test must always be applied. Because true miracle-workers are inspired as to their teaching, their doctrine may be presumed to be correct. That means it will conform exactly to biblical revelation.

But sometimes there is a misunderstanding of what John is saying. There are those who think that you must test every teacher concerning his belief about whether or not Jesus came in the flesh. While that may not be a bad thing in itself, it is not the test that John had in mind. Obviously, there are cults and sects who believe that truth,[2] but who teach other things that are erroneous. What, then, was John saying?

The dominant heresy that John was confronting in his letter was a form of Gnosticism that denied the physical reality of Jesus' body. This error grew out of the Gnostic belief that matter is evil. Obviously, then, if Jesus' body was fleshly, it would be evil. The Gnostic error existed in two forms. One form said that Jesus had only a phantom body, not a physical one. To say that it was a phantom body—i.e., had but the "appearance" of a body—would relieve the Gnostic of his problem. The other Gnostic dodge was to claim that the man Jesus had a physical body, but that "the Christ" came upon him at the baptism but left before the cross.[3] So the man Jesus was not the Christ. Both of these views are heretical, and John refutes them by giving the doctrinal test that would expose the error: Does the teacher believe Jesus Christ came in the flesh?

However, that all applied to the Gnostic heresy. What of other heresies? The specific test for Gnosticism is mentioned in 1 John 4:2-3. But the general test (of which the Gnostic test is but one application) is found in 1 John 4:6: "We are of God; whoever knows God listens to us, but whoever isn't of God doesn't listen to us. From this we know the spirit of truth and the spirit of error." In other words, since the apostles (the "we" of 4:6) were clearly from God, and their message was His message, whoever disagreed with that apostolic message proved himself not to be from God. He was a false prophet.[4]

---

2   For instance, the Roman church, the world's largest sect, believes Jesus came in the flesh.
3   John refutes this belief in 1 John 5:6 where he declares that He was the Christ not only when He was baptized but also when He died: He came not only by water, but also by blood.
4   Obviously, the apostolic message consisted of more teaching than that of

So, the ultimate test was not whether one performed miracles or not (though, together with true teaching, miracles formed a valuable service in authenticating God's servants); it was whether he taught in accordance with apostolic teaching. A claim about the miraculous would alert the New Testament Christian, it is true, but that was not enough. He then had to examine whether that claim held up, by determining whether any prophecies connected with it came to pass and by determining whether the supposed prophet's teaching conformed to that of the apostles.

Today, the situation is somewhat different, as we have seen. The very fact that one claims to do signs and wonders *dis*authenticates him. We must immediately turn from him. We know that his teaching is false, because he attempts to reproduce the situation that existed in the apostolic age, even though there are no apostles alive and no new revelation to be authenticated. The completeness of the Bible and its sufficiency for the church today (containing "everything for life and godliness," 2 Peter 1:3) make the very claims of signs and wonders suspect from the outset. If someone claims to be true to the apostolic word today, he will *deny* that he performs the "signs of an apostle," and he will *deny* that there are any reve-latory gifts still operational. To *affirm* these things is, thereby, to disqualify his claims.

---

the fleshly coming of Jesus Christ.

CHAPTER 6

A CHARISMATIC ERA

I**F**, indeed, the books of the New Testament were written prior to 70 AD during the apostolic period, what should we expect to find in them? Remember what Joel predicted:

> *On the contrary, this is what the prophet Joel spoke about:*
> *In the last days, God says,*
> *I will pour out My Spirit on all flesh,*
> *and your sons and your daughters will prophesy,*
> *your young men will see visions,*
> *and your old men will dream dreams;*
> *and even on My male and female slaves I will*
> *pour out My Spirit in those days, and they will prophesy.*
> *I will perform wonders in the sky above*
> *and signs on the earth below—blood and fire and clouds of smoke.*
> *The sun will be darkened and the moon turned to blood*
> *before the great and glorious day of the Lord comes.*
> *Everybody who calls on the Lord's name will be saved.*
>
> *(Acts 2:16-21)*

Since that was to be the condition that would persist throughout the forty-year period, we would expect to find the exercise of spiritual gifts in full swing. And, as Joel rightly predicted, that is precisely what we find.

The Charismatics taunt us for not having such gifts in operation in our churches today, pointing to those which we read about in the book of Acts and the epistles. But we are not embarrassed at all in discovering that in New Testament times the charismata are present in abundance. Indeed, were they not evident during that period, we might have to doubt the accuracy of the Scriptures. Signs and wonders characterized not only the ministry of the Lord Jesus Christ, but also that of His apostles. The period is replete with the miraculous. But what of our day? Where can we find any biblical prediction of miracles in our time? There are none. Thus there is no reason for us to expect them.

We are delighted that these gifts occurred in New Testament times. They mean that our faith was well attested, as we have seen. Jesus was accredited "by miracles and wonders and signs that God performed" (Acts 2:22). The apostles, following Jesus' death and resurrection, performed even "greater" (i.e., more extensive) "works" (miracles) in His Name (John 14:12; Acts 3:6; 4:10, 12, 18). Throughout their ministries, we have every biblical reason to think that the apostles continued to do signs and wonders in His Name:

> *12 Now many signs and wonders were performed among the people by the hands of the apostles. And they all used to meet with one mind in Solomon's portico. 13 But the rest didn't dare to join them; yet the people spoke highly of them, 14 and more than ever believers were added to the Lord, great throngs of men and women. 15 They actually brought the sick out into the streets and put them on beds and mats, so that as Peter went by his shadow might fall on some of them. 16 A crowd also came together from the cities round about Jerusalem, bringing the sick and those who were tormented by unclean spirits, and they were all healed.*

> (Acts 5:12-16)

Now, not only the apostles, but also the deacons performed wonders. We are told, for instance, that Stephen "did great wonders and signs among the people" (Acts 6:8). And he was empowered to preach the longest sermon recorded by Luke in Acts, at the conclusion of which he was stoned to death. But, note well, what preceded his death was a miraculous vision of the ascended and reigning Savior that, to the consternation of the rulers, he described to his listeners:

> *But he, full of the Holy Spirit, gazed at the sky and saw God's glory and Jesus standing at God's right hand, and said, "There, I see the heavens opened up, and the Son of Man standing at God's right*

hand!" Then they shouted with a loud voice and covered their ears and rushed on him with one thought in mind. They threw him out of the city and stoned him. And the witnesses took off their clothes and laid them at the feet of a young man named Saul. As they were stoning Stephen, he prayed, saying, "Lord Jesus, receive my spirit." Then he knelt down and shouted with a loud voice, "Lord, don't hold this sin against them!" And when he had said this, he fell asleep.

(Acts 7:55-60)

Having tasted blood, the religious leaders began to persecute the church in earnest. A great persecution in Jerusalem, spearheaded by Saul (who was later to become the apostle Paul) broke out, driving the Christians who lived there out of the city into safer places. There they carried the gospel message and many in other places believed.[1]

Philip, another deacon, also performed miracles in Samaria:

The crowds unitedly paid attention to the things Philip said when they heard and saw the signs he was performing. Unclean spirits, shouting with a loud voice, came out of many of those who had been possessed by them, and many paralytics and lame persons were healed. So there was much joy in that city.

(Acts 8:6-8)

Simon, a magician, was so impressed by the miraculous nature of the apostles' ministry, that he wished to buy the power to confer the Holy Spirit and His gifts by the laying on of hands. Clearly, word of what Peter and John were doing had spread widely, because their miraculous power had great impact.

Throughout the book of Acts we read about special revelation of the sort given to Philip by an angel (Acts 8:26), and even directly by the Spirit Himself (Acts 8:29). Even on one occasion, in some extraordinary manner, the Spirit "snatched Philip away" from the Gaza area and transported him to Azotus (Acts 8:39-40).

The conversion of Saul is no less miraculous (Acts 9). It happened by means of an actual appearance of the risen Lord on the road to

---

1   In His wise providence God used Paul to spread the gospel even before his conversion!

Damascus. The blindness and subsequent healing that Saul received, along with the impartation of the Spirit by the laying on of Ananias' hands (Acts 9:17), were additional miraculous incidents. Moreover, Peter's vision of the great tarp let down from heaven containing the unclean animals, with the revelation concerning the "cleansing" of the Gentiles that accompanied it, stressed the miraculous nature of God's dealings with His early church (Acts 10:9-28). And so it continues throughout the book of Acts.

We find accounts of such things in the epistles as well. When writing to the Romans, Paul spoke of the miraculous ministry he conducted:

> ... *by the power of signs and wonders, by the power of the Holy Spirit, so that from Jerusalem and all around as far as Illyricum, I have fully preached the good news about Christ.*
>
> *(Romans 15:19)*

We have mentioned already the plethora of gifts that the Corinthian church enjoyed (1 Corinthians 1:7), and the Galatians had known "miracles" in their midst as well (Galatians 3:5). The Thessalonians had received predictions that were fulfilled (1 Thessalonians 3:4) and were also the recipients of prophecies (1 Thessalonians 5:20-21). Individuals experienced wonders. For instance, Timothy's call to the ministry took place in response to a revelation (1 Timothy 4:14), and he was fully informed about Paul's supernatural experiences as well (2 Timothy 4:17).

These limited samples show beyond question that Joel's description of the "last days" was perfectly accurate. The period was characterized by extraordinary events. It was a truly charismatic time!

But what I want to ask is whether the kinds of things that Cymbala and others promote in any way measure up to what we see in the New Testament. Do you think that they do? Look at the Scriptural record; then look at what the average charismatic offers today. People are lined up on the stage and shuffled past the "healer" as if they were going through a car wash! He may speak a word to them or strike them on the head. Then they are led off the platform. I remember once being in such a meeting. There was disorder of the most pronounced sort; people were wandering here and there around the place. Since everyone else was, I went up on the stage also to get a closer look at what was happening. The "healer" shook an old woman who was crippled from head to foot with arthritis, then, pronouncing her healed, he went on to the next person in line. I followed the woman across the platform, helped her down the steps, and inquired about how she felt. She was in excruciating agony. She wasn't healed at all, even though she had been pronounced healed. "Ah," you say, "She didn't have faith!" Of course, that is the typical dodge. But, I ask you, did she have faith? The answer is yes; great faith. I had to drive this woman home because she had spent her last bit of money to get a cab to take her to the meeting. She wasn't even concerned about how she would get home! She thought if she was going to be healed, she would be able to walk! Now, that's faith for you. The problem wasn't faith; the problem was that her faith was placed in the wrong object!

Then there are the even wilder scenes that come from some charismatic churches. People bark like dogs, are supposedly slain in the Spirit, and make fools of themselves with so-called "holy laughter." Does any of this align with—even remotely—the New Testament narratives?

No. There is a wonderful, orderly, exciting (but sane) miraculous element that pervades the apostolic era. There are none of the absurdities that characterize modern movements that purport to duplicate that era. The similarity soon evaporates when one carefully compares what transpires in the two times. Today's charismatic cannot pull it off! He has bitten off more than he can chew. He is unable to reproduce the wonderful miracle-studded pages of the New Testament—no matter how hard he tries. Where are the dead who have been raised? Where are those blind from birth who now see? Where is the person with an amputated arm who, in response to a healer's word, sprouts a brand new one? Instead, we hear of such ridiculous things as fillings in teeth turning to gold!

Consider once more the reason why New Testament miracles occurred: to authenticate the revelatory message preached and the messenger. Clearly, modern "miracle-workers" can show no such purpose in what they do. While Peter heals after saying "silver and gold have I none," today's healer is likely to haul both in by the basketful. The differences between the two couldn't be more obvious. If one has any objectivity at all, he cannot help but conclude that modern claims consist of nothing more than sham and self-deceit.

Furthermore, so much of what happened in New Testament times was in fulfillment of Old Testament prophecy. You see this in Acts 2, as Joel's prophecy came to pass. Peter, Stephen, and Paul all pointed out that the things that were happening were in direct fulfillment of the predictions of the coming Messiah. No charismatic today, no matter how great his boast, can claim to be fulfilling Messianic prophecy. He can't come near!

So I ask you, "How can you put faith in modern-day claims— even if you had nothing more to base your judgment upon than a comparison of the present with the apostolic period?" Think about this. What is offered today is but an insipid parody of the real thing.

Thank God, then, that in apostolic times there was a charismatic era. Because of it, we know Christianity is true, since it was well-attested, and we know modern charismatic claims are not true—for the very same reason.

W E have already touched on the matter of prophecy in several other chapters, but there is one aspect of the matter that is quite pertinent to the present discussion. The apostolic age (the "last days" of Joel's prophecy) was a period that was specially predicted in the Old Testament, as shown by Joel's words quoted by Peter on the Day of Pentecost. Those days were the times of the Messiah and His apostles, who were engaged in establishing the new kingdom of the heavens. Those were the times when the kingdom would be extended to all the nations, as many Old Testament prophecies had predicted. That those days had been singled out from past times as unique, then, is significant.

Jesus' entire life and ministry was characterized by the fulfillment of prophecy. Again and again the writers of the Gospels point out this fact (see, for example, Matthew 1:22; 2:5-6, 17-18; 3:3; 4:14). Many have commented that the life of Christ could almost be sketched from prophecy alone. In a way quite different from anything that we experience today, the end of an age had come; a new age had dawned. Events were taking place "in the fullness of time" (Galatians 4:4); God was "sending forth His Son" Who would establish a new covenant (Jeremiah 31:31-34). Those days were of exceedingly great interest long before they dawned: Jesus said that this was the time that "many prophets and kings wanted to see … but didn't" (Luke 10:24). Clearly, those were not ordinary times!

Moreover, these were to be times of revelation. Paul spoke of the apostles and prophets as a "foundational" gift to the early church (Ephesians 2:20). It was through them that, after so many years of silence, new revelation would be given (Ephesians 3:5). Indeed, describing his own ministry, he wrote:

> Now to the One Who is able to strengthen you by my gospel, even the proclamation about Jesus Christ, according to the revelation of the secret that was kept quiet for ages, but now has been disclosed by order of the eternal God, and through the prophetic Scriptures has been made known to all the Gentiles to bring about obedience by faith.…
>
> (Romans 16:25-26)

Paul speaks of the revelation as, in part, "the secret that was kept quiet for ages." That means that this secret about the Gentiles being received into God's covenant people was a focal point of the "ages." People in past times didn't understand exactly what would happen or how it would take place. All of that had become an open secret in the apostolic age. There was no more waiting to find out.

In ages past there were prophecies about the Savior-Messiah. People longed for those days and hoped that they would come in their lifetimes. At last, those cherished times had appeared. These were the times to which Old Testament believers were taught to look forward:

> … but with Christ's valuable blood, shed like the blood of a spotless and unblemished lamb. He was foreknown, indeed, before the foundation of a world, but at these last times He made His appearance for your sake who through Him have believed in God, Who raised Him from the dead and gave Him glory, so that your faith and hope are in God.
>
> (1 Peter 1:19-21)

And Jesus said, "Abraham was delighted at the prospect of seeing My day; and he saw it and rejoiced" (John 8:56).

John the Baptist was the last of the Old Testament prophets. As Jesus told us, "all the prophets and the law prophesied until John" (Matthew 11:13). With him, an era ended and a new one began. He stood on the razor's edge between two ages.[2] There was to be no

---

2   Jesus distinguished between John, the greatest of Old Testament prophets, and the humblest believer today, who is "least in the empire from the heavens" but who is "greater than [John] is" (Matthew 11:11). The era was what made

more of such prophecy. The last days of the Old Testament era had come. Old Testament prophecies of the coming of Christ and His empire (kingdom) were now being fulfilled.

That was why John and Jesus came announcing that the empire from the heavens was "at hand" (Matthew 3:2; Mark 1:15), and it is why Paul preached that it had come (Acts 28:31). The fact is, it was about to be inaugurated when John and Jesus preached it, and it came in its fullness when Jesus was declared both Lord and Christ at His resurrection, ascension, and coronation (Acts 2:36). The empire (or kingdom) of which they were speaking was the long-awaited one predicted in Old Testament prophecy. In recounting Nebuchadnezzar's dream, Daniel described this empire as the everlasting fifth world-kingdom that, like a growing stone, would fill the whole earth:

> *31 You, O king, were looking and behold, there was a single great statue; that statue, which was large and of extraordinary splendor, was standing in front of you, and its appearance was awesome. 32 The head of that statue was made of fine gold, its breast and its arms of silver, its belly and its thighs of bronze, 33 its legs of iron, its feet partly of iron and partly of clay. 34 You continued looking until a stone was cut out without hands, and it struck the statue on its feet of iron and clay and crushed them. 35 Then the iron, the clay, the bronze, the silver and the gold were crushed all at the same time and became like chaff from the summer threshing floors; and the wind carried them away so that not a trace of them was found. But the stone that struck the statue became a great mountain and filled the whole earth.*
>
> *(Daniel 2:31-35)*

---

the difference, not the persons involved in the comparison and contrast. John's knowledge of the new era was deficient. The least member of God's empire today knows more about the life, the death and the resurrection of Christ. John and his disciples wore old garments that couldn't be patched and the truth they contained was in old wineskins that could not be used for the new wine of the kingdom. They simply were not a part of the new era. The New Testament believer not only had new and greater knowledge, but also privileges far exceeding John's.

The metallic image pictured in the book of Daniel was prophetic of the various world-empires that would hold sway over the years to come. First, there was the Babylonian empire, which was in ascendancy when Daniel wrote. This empire would be followed by the Medo-Persian empire that, under Cyrus, would defeat Babylon. Then, under Alexander the Great, the Greek empire would extend over an even greater territory. But even this empire would give way to the Roman empire, which was destined to rule the *oikoumene* (or civilized world) of New Testament times. The Roman empire was to be the final empire in the metallic image succession.

In the days of Rome's rule, however, a fifth empire would appear. It would be unlike the first four in several respects. First, it would not be given over to another world power as each of the preceding empires had been. Instead, it would last forever. Second, it would not be an empire that was built by the efforts of some great statesman or warrior. Indeed, no mere human being would set it up. Pictured under the figure of a stone quarried from a mountain "without hands"[3] which would strike the feet of the image and bring the whole crashing down, this empire would be given to the Messiah, the Son of Man.

This giving of the everlasting empire to the Son of Man was depicted in greater detail as part of Daniel's dream in chapter 7 that parallels Nebuchadnezzar's dream:

"I kept looking in the night visions,
And behold, with the clouds of heaven
One like a Son of Man was coming,
And He came up to the Ancient of Days
And was presented before Him.
"And to Him was given dominion,
Glory and a kingdom,
That all the peoples, nations and men of every language
Might serve Him.
His dominion is an everlasting dominion

---

3   That is, the empire would be not of human but of divine origin.

Which will not pass away;
And His kingdom is one
Which will not be destroyed."

(Daniel 7:13-14)

The interpretation of Daniel's dream includes still further detail of the ascendance of God's everlasting empire over the same four world-empires (now pictured as four beasts):

> "*Then I desired to know the exact meaning of the fourth beast, which was different from all the others, exceedingly dreadful, with its teeth of iron and its claws of bronze, and which devoured, crushed and trampled down the remainder with its feet, and the meaning of the ten horns that were on its head and the other horn which came up, and before which three of them fell, namely, that horn which had eyes and a mouth uttering great boasts and which was larger in appearance than its associates. I kept looking, and that horn was waging war with the saints and overpowering them until the Ancient of Days came and judgment was passed in favor of the saints of the Highest One, and the time arrived when the saints took possession of the kingdom. Thus he said: 'The fourth beast will be a fourth kingdom on the earth, which will be different from all the other kingdoms and will devour the whole earth and tread it down and crush it. As for the ten horns, out of this kingdom ten kings will arise; and another will arise after them, and he will be different from the previous ones and will subdue three kings. He will speak out against the Most High and wear down the saints of the Highest One, and he will intend to make alterations in times and in law; and they will be given into his hand for a time, times, and half a time. But the court will sit for judgment, and his dominion will be taken away, annihilated and destroyed forever. Then the sovereignty, the dominion and the greatness of all the kingdoms under the whole heaven will be given to the people of the saints of the Highest One; His kingdom will be an everlasting kingdom, and all the dominions will serve and obey Him.' "*

(Daniel 7:19-27)

These prophecies came to pass in the days of the Lord Jesus Christ. Daniel 7:13 is an important passage that must not be missed in passing or misunderstood because of some preconceived notions. Too frequently people either pass over the verse or misapply it. The reference in that verse is *not* to the second coming of Christ as some have supposed. That Jesus is pictured coming with a cloud is no indication that the coming Daniel has in view is the second coming. Deity is frequently represented as moving to and fro in the company of clouds (cf. Ex. 19:16-20; Psalm 99:7; 104:3; Is. 19:1; Ez. 1:4, 26-28; Mk. 9:7; Rev. 14:14). So the fact that a cloud is mentioned tells us nothing about the direction of the movement of the One like the "Son of Man" whose coming is recorded.

Some seem to respond only one way to the word "coming" whenever they encounter it in the Bible. They think only of Jesus' second advent. But it is clear from the passage itself that it refers not to movement toward the earth, but to movement that took place from one place to another in the heavens. Daniel 7:13 explicitly says that the Messiah was coming *"to* the Ancient of Days" (i.e., to God the Father), not to the *earth.* This coming is quite meaningful in light of the number of New Testament references to it.

But what was the purpose of this heavenly coming? Why did the Messiah advance toward the Ancient of Days? What happened when He arrived at His destination? He was advancing to receive an empire from the Father's hand. This was Daniel's fifth empire that would never pass away or be given to another. This was the time of the coronation of Christ predicted in Psalm 2:6-9:[1]

> *"But as for Me, I have installed My King upon Zion, My holy mountain. I will surely tell of the decree of the Lord: He said to Me, 'You are My Son, Today I have begotten You. Ask of Me, and I will surely give the nations as Your inheritance, and the very ends of the earth as Your possession. You shall break them with a rod of iron, You shall shatter them like earthenware.' "*

---

1   Cf. Hebrews 5:5. To "beget" a son in such a context is regal language for declaring one a ruler.

Daniel and the Psalmist refer to what happened after Jesus ascended in the cloud (Acts 1:9). You might say that they previewed events that would happen on the other side of the ascension cloud.[2]

The kingdom that John and Jesus announced was "at hand," and that Paul preached as having come was the Messianic fifth kingdom of Daniel's prophecy which was to commence in the days of the Roman empire. And the kingdom arrived right on schedule! This kingdom (or world-empire) was given to "the saints of the Most High" who would possess it forever (Daniel 7:18; cf. 7:27). This was the empire to which Jesus referred in Matthew 16:19. It was the kingdom over which He was crowned Ruler in fulfillment of Psalm 8:

> *And somebody at some place has testified:*
> **What is man that You remember him**
> **or a son of man that You should take care of him?**
> **You made him for a short time lower than the angels;**
> **You crowned him with glory and honor**
> **and subjected everything beneath his feet.**
> *And, in subjecting "everything" to him, He didn't leave anything that isn't subject to him. Of course, at the present time we don't see everything subject to him. But we do see Jesus, Who for a short time was made lower than the angels, crowned with glory and honor because He suffered death, so that by God's grace He might taste death for all sorts of people.*
>
> *(Hebrews 2:6–9)*

All of this testimony to the extraordinary nature of the last days should help the serious student to understand that these were not times like ours. They were radically different. The signs and wonders that occurred were not only to testify to the messenger, but also, as

---

2   Throughout the New Testament there are references to seeing Jesus coming on clouds of heaven (Matthew 24:29-30; Mark 13:23-26; Luke 21:25-27, etc.). These passages (and others like them) use the language of Daniel 7 because they refer to the fulfillment of that prophecy. They speak of Jesus' coronation as the Ruler over His worldwide empire. As He was about to ascend to receive the crown of rule in forty days, proleptically He declared "all authority in heaven and in earth has been given to Me" (Matthew 28:18).

we have seen, to the message. A significant teaching that was a part of that message was that the Savior had risen from the dead and, subsequently, had taken His place on the throne at the Father's right hand, where He would jointly rule over heaven and earth as the God-man. That was no light fact; so it took miracles to attest to and fulfilled prophecies to verify the claim. In Christ, because of the ascension of His glorified body, humanity is now seated on the throne of the universe!

Notice how Jesus Himself attached the verification of His teaching to His power to work miracles: "If I cast out demons by God's finger,[3] then God's empire has come upon you" (Luke 11:20). In other words, the miracle was evidence of the coming of Daniel's empire from the heavens.[4] These miracles attested to the fact that the fulfillment of prophecy was at hand (it had "come upon" them as if it were already there).

Now, in the light of our study, what does all of this mean? These facts are further evidence that the era in which Jesus lived and died, and the forty years' extension of that period (the apostolic age), was unique. Our age does not correspond to it at all. It was an age of great transition (as we saw earlier) when one might expect unique events and powers to be at work. Anyone who wants to equate our times with the times of Jesus and the apostles will find his work cut out for him! Indeed, our day is so unlike those days that we can hardly compare them. Those who see no distinction between the periods in question, it seems, must attach a certain importance

---

3   That is, God's power given through the Holy Spirit (cf. Matthew 12:28, where "Spirit" is equated with "finger." It is possible that the Spirit, Who executes God's will, is anthropomorphically thought of as the hand of God by which He does so).

4   Casting out demons, in particular, was evidence of the power of God that would establish Jesus on the throne, since it demonstrated the fact that Jesus had come to destroy and despoil the kingdom of Satan (Hebrews 2:14-15; Matthew 12:28-29). Daniel's four world-empires represent different manifestations of the one Satanic kingdom (the image consisted of differing metals, but was one image). Jesus' universal empire from the heavens like the stone cut out of the mountains without hands (which had no human origin), would smash the metallic image, putting an end to Satanic world-dominion (cf. Col. 2:13-15).

to themselves (as if they were entitled to the very same God-given abilities that Jesus and His apostles were). But they simply cannot justify doing so from the scriptural record. There is nothing unique about our times that calls for miraculous, attesting gifts of the Spirit. It is not an age in which prophecy is being fulfilled. No wonder that among people who lay claim to signs and wonders today, we often find many who arrogate to themselves an undue importance that ought not be assumed by any servant of God (Luke 9:46-48). It is, therefore, of the utmost significance to recognize the vast difference in times. If the charismatics were able to show convincing evidence that their movement is the fulfillment of biblical prophecy, as were the events of the Gospel and apostolic ages, we might begin to seriously consider their claims. But, of course, they cannot.

CHAPTER 8
HERE'S HOW IT WORKS

So far, I have tried to show that the special gifts that were so prevalent during the apostolic age have ceased. There is no longer a need for them since their purpose—to attest to the prophet and the new revelation he brought—has also ceased. We must consider this fact in interpreting and applying the Scriptures. I have shown that we should do this by discovering the universal principles in any given passage that have broader implications than in that particular context.

We saw, for example, how the apostle Paul did this very thing when he applied material from Israel's apostasy in the wilderness directly to the Corinthian church (1 Corinthians 10). Then we considered how, by extracting a principle from the law given to regulate the way in which owners should treat their oxen, he was able to show that the underlying principle applies with even greater validity to meeting the financial needs of Christian workers. In this way it is possible to understand God's will for us today without becoming confused about outmoded circumstances that might otherwise make us shy away from a given scriptural passage.

As clear as these examples may be, it still might be of service to take a look at some other passages where we might particularly have difficulty because of the thick miraculous element that overlies the principles which are involved.

Let me begin by quoting from my commentary on 1 Corinthians 12:4-26 in the *Christian Counselor's Commentary* series.

> In verses 4-26, Paul explains that Jesus gave the early church different kinds of gifts through the laying on of his hands and focuses on the purpose for which they were given. In verses 4-6 he says that:
> 1) gifts differ (v. 4), 2) their purposes differ (v. 5) and 3) the results

of their uses differ (v. 6). Yet the same Spirit gives them all. In other words, the Holy Spirit is sovereign in the ways in which He disperses gifts.

This sovereign dispensation of gifts by the Spirit contains an important principle for counselors. God is the One Who brings about the differences among us. Therefore, we should neither complain nor boast about our abilities and accomplishments. After all, as Paul notes, anything worthwhile is accomplished by God through you (v. 6b).[5]

The large "principle" in the passage is as applicable to the use of ordinary gifts as it is to extraordinary ones. And I think that you will agree that the application is no less powerful, even though when I wrote, I assumed that no reader would possess miraculous gifts like those in view in the chapter. If I had brought the miraculous fully into the discussion, I might have easily confused the reader. Indeed, doing so in itself might be the cause of unnecessary difficulty since the reader would realize that he doesn't have extraordinary gifts and might exempt himself from God's requirements in the passage.

Commenting later, on verses 8 through 10, I observed

… that these are all extraordinary gifts and, therefore, are "foundational" (Eph. 2:20; 3:5). The critical fact is found in verse 11. The Holy Spirit produced them in the members of the church *as He determined.*[6]

Here, I tried to help the reader see that it is not necessary to have miraculous gifts in order to understand the "critical fact" found in verse 11. That fact, the sovereign distribution of varying gifts from the Spirit, in no way depends on the possession of *special* gifts from Him. Touching on the matter of extraordinary gifts, however, and showing where the subject might be addressed more fully (in the commentary on Ephesians 2:20; 3:5), I continued on, stressing the primary emphasis of the chapter. God's purpose in these verses, therefore, may be recognized apart from an in-depth discussion of the special gift problem.

---

5   *The Christian Counselors Commentary: I & II Corinthians.*
6   Ibid., p. 78.

1 Corinthians 13:1-8 is easily applied apart from much concern about special gifts, even though it is found in the midst of Paul's argument about those gifts and their use. Then comes the section that I have already dealt with in this book about the cessation of knowledge, tongues, and prophecy (vv. 9–13). Because these verses have been expounded earlier, I shall pass over them in this place and move on to the more problematic chapter 14.

Without quoting from my comments on chapter 14 in the commentary, let me simply point out how the fundamental principles upon which Paul bases his argument are every bit as valuable to us today, even though we may study and apply them apart from special gifts. The first verse urges us to desire gifts from the Spirit, stressing that we should make a distinction among those gifts that we desire. Here, he says, *"especially* that you may prophesy." This is a direct statement that the Corinthians should especially wish to gain the gift of prophecy. If we should not expect to receive the prophetic gift today, how do we follow that advice? Surely there are those who go astray right at that point.

Because the recommendation is there—clear and plain—some think that they must seek the gift of prophecy. And there are plenty of people out there who will encourage them to do so. But, to echo the phraseology of Paul when he spoke about oxen, may we not similarly ask, "Was Paul speaking about prophesying?" The answer is yes and no. Yes, with reference to the immediate situation in Corinth, where the choices in the discussion seem to have narrowed to two: tongues or prophecy. But we are reading and learning from the passage today in an era in which those very gifts have ceased and been done away with. What do we do then? How do we obey the biblical injunction?

Well, let's be clear about what Paul is actually saying. It is not prophecy, in particular, that we should desire—especially since God has "set aside" prophecy! But given the choice between prophecy (which edifies when used in church meetings) and tongues (which do not, unless interpreted), it would be wise to desire prophecy over tongues. Why? As Paul says in the next verses, tongues (foreign languages) are not understood (except as God did) by those who do not speak them. But the purpose of the tongue is to speak to people who can understand that language in order to lead them to faith in Jesus Christ. But prophecy is understood because it is given in one's own language and, as a result, those who hear are edified, "encouraged" and "comforted" (or exhorted).7 In other words, one should desire those gifts that prove most profitable to others. Now, there is a principle that we may use today. It extends to the use of all God-given gifts, including the ordinary ones that we have. We should seek to acquire, develop, and utilize those abilities that are useful for others, rather than those which are esoteric or that benefit only ourselves. The passage is not irrelevant, therefore, simply because the age of special gifts has passed.

In verses 13 through 19, Paul drives home another important principle: all that we do for God ought to be a matter of *intelligible* effort on our part. The mind must not be bypassed in worship. There are, for instance, many who are addicted to emotionalism in corporate worship. That is tragic. As a result, they give little or no thought to the theology expressed in the hymns that they sing. If the tune is pleasant, singable, or memorable, to them, that's all that counts! But no; before God it isn't all that counts. The "mind," says Paul, must be involved for anyone to be edified by what is spoken or sung. Hymns must be chosen for faithful, biblical content, as well as for singability. That critical principle, involved in what one does in corporate worship, grows out of Paul's discussion of special gifts. As you can see, it has value for us since its application is not dependent on the possession of spiritual gifts like speaking in tongues or prophecy. The principle is broader and, therefore, much more widely applicable. At the conclusion of verse 26, the important principle that lies beneath the surface of all that Paul is teaching here emerges: "be sure that everything builds up" (edifies).

Next we encounter another significant matter in corporate worship: everything should be done "decently and in order" (v.

---

7   The word *parakaleo* can mean both things.

40). There are many ways to cause disorder in church meetings. In Corinth, some of those involved the use of extraordinary spiritual gifts. The way in which Paul deals with several of these from verse 26 to the end of the chapter leads to this important conclusion about decency and order. Prophetic speaking, for instance, should be done "in turn," he insists (v. 27). In verses 29 through 31, it is clear that no two people (or more) should speak at the same time. There should be no hubbub in which many speak at once.

Then, having received a prophetic revelation, the other prophets should "judge" the revelation. That doesn't mean that they should judge its truth or falsity. God's revelations need no such verification by others! The judging has to do with what it means to the church, or to those specifically involved. They should judge as to its import. They should make judgments about how to apply the revelation in their church situation.

And this orderly method of proceeding must not be violated by some prophet maintaining that he cannot help but speak, even though by doing so he interrupts another. He cannot plead special urgency for doing it, as if what he has to say is more important than what someone else is saying. Nor may he plead that he is in some sort of uncontrollable ecstasy; his spirit is "subject" to his mind (v. 32); he is perfectly capable of exercising control over what he does and says. Otherwise, there would be "confusion" (v. 33). Here you see how the principle of *order* is once again emphasized by denying the necessity for its opposite.[8]

In addition, order is maintained when women keep silent in the meetings rather than calling out for answers to questions that they should discuss with their husbands at home. Presumably, they were a disorderly bunch who were breaking up the proper flow of things by these questions, thereby causing much confusion. Such disorder was not to be tolerated in any of the churches (v. 33). This rule is not for Corinth alone. That principle is also important: today, churches

---

8   Compare this to the disorder caused by people moaning and screaming, others falling on the floor, barking, etc.

have no warrant for sloppy services, confusion, and disorder, even under the guise of allowing the Spirit to run things. Here we see what it is that pleases the Spirit—order, not confusion.[1]

There is even an incidental, but very valuable principle to be learned from verses 37 and 38. Anyone who disregards the prophetic word, disregards God Himself. The word that Paul is writing in this place, he says, is *God's* Word—*His* "commandment." Paul was not merely giving his own opinion but God's Word. That fact affirms not only the doctrine of inerrancy—*God's* Word is never in error—but also the authority of the Scriptures. Plainly, fundamental principles that focus on order, on edification, and on concern about cultivating abilities that help others are principles that remain for us today. Many need to heed them!

We have learned from this brief survey of an admittedly supernatural portion of Scripture that it is every bit as applicable to us as it was to the Corinthians. We have also learned that extracting the principle from the particular situation is not all that difficult. We have learned that biblical passages have purposes that are larger than the application given in a particular passage.

Let's now turn to a narrative portion in the book of Acts to see how this method works there. Before considering a specific passage, however, it is important to observe that an epistle, in which Paul is correcting and guiding a congregation, is very different from a narrative that is written to an individual (Theophilus) in order to inform him about what "Jesus continued to do and teach until the day that He was taken up" (Acts 1:1-2). Acts was the second installment of a two-part narrative that continued what had been begun in the book of Luke. In the preface to the entire two-part series, Luke wrote,

> *Since a number of persons have undertaken the task of compiling an account of the events that have most certainly taken place in our midst just as they were handed down to us by those who from the*

---

1   Regardless of Cymbala's plea for "spontaneity" (p.148), in which expected sermons may be replaced by prayer, etc.

*outset became eyewitnesses and ministers of the Word, it seemed good
for me too, because I had thoroughly investigated everything from its
beginning, to write an orderly account for you, most excellent Theophilus, so that you might know the reliability of the facts in which
you have been instructed.   (Luke 1:1-4)*

As you can see, his purpose was very different from Paul's in
writing an epistle such as 1 Corinthians. Keeping that in mind,
you should look for an accurate account in Luke and Acts of the
ministry of Jesus Christ, first carried on personally and then from
the heavens by means of the Holy Spirit, Who worked through
some of the apostles.[2]

The reliability and adequacy of the material that Luke presents is
uppermost in his mind. In the midst of the confusing and possibly
inaccurate accounts by others, he wants Theophilus to know the
truth. So in the book of Acts, as in the Gospel, Luke goes to lengths
to gather the facts from trustworthy witnesses and to present them
in an "orderly account" (Luke 1:3). Throughout, of course, there
are sub-purposes woven into the book.[3]

With those observations in mind, let us consider the third chapter
of Acts, where we read of the miraculous healing of a cripple who had
been "lame from birth" (v. 2). The man was well known by all as he
begged at the gates of the temple. When he asked for money, Peter
said that he had none, but that he would give him what he could. This
turned out to be something more valuable than gold—healing from
his lifelong affliction. In Christ's name he commanded the cripple to
walk (v. 6). He did, and then went walking, jumping, and praising
God throughout the temple grounds (v. 8). The people recognized
him, saw what had happened, and were amazed (vv. 9-10).

Because he "clung to Peter and John," people quickly gathered
around them (v. 11). Obviously, they wanted to know precisely what

---

2   Obviously, the Spirit worked through all of them, but Acts records only
the ministry of the three (Peter, John and Paul) who carried the gospel to
Rome following the three-part outline that Christ laid out in Acts 1:8.
3   For instance, how the Spirit led the apostles to adapt to various sorts of
audiences (cf. footnote 1 on p. 81).

had happened to heal him and how it took place. Peter was quite willing to respond to their questions (v. 12) and he took advantage of the occasion to deliver a message to them (vv. 12-26). In that Spirit-inspired message Peter explained that Jesus, Whom they crucified and Whom God raised from the dead, had performed the miracle by means of faith (vv. 13-16). This faith was centered in Jesus' Name.[4]

Then, Peter went on to show that out of ignorance of the Old Testament prophecies, which were fulfilled by Jesus, they did what they did to Him. He called upon them to repent and turn from their sins for forgiveness (vv.18-19). If they did, he assured them, they would receive times (seasons) of "refreshing" (relief from the toils of sin), and some day they would again see Jesus, Who would be sent from the heavens after all was "restored" to God's good order. All of this, again, Peter further assured them, had happened (and would happen) exactly the way that God foretold through His prophets (vv. 20-21).

In conclusion, he reminded them that God promised to send a prophet like Moses who had to be heard. Whoever refused to listen would be excluded from the people of God (vv. 22-23). And he explained that it was not only Moses' prophecy that spoke of Christ, but "the prophets ... as many as spoke, also announced these days" (v. 24).[5] Then Peter cited the Abrahamic promise as being fulfilled in Jesus (v. 25) and called upon them as Jews, who had been the first to hear of the coming Messiah, to continue in the covenant promises by repenting and believing (v. 26).

Now there is much of the miraculous in the story that is recorded. But clearly, it was recorded for our instruction who are living in these post-apostolic times. How may we "translate" it into profit and blessing for ourselves?

First, remember that the main purpose of Acts is to assure the reader that he is in possession of an accurate, orderly account of

---

4   That is, He is Jesus (Savior) Christ (Messiah).
5   Once more, we see evidence of the prophetic concern that marked out these days as special. Again, we must emphasize the vast difference between Peter's time and our own.

what Jesus was continuing to do and say from heaven. The details that are given, the finesse with which Luke handles his materials, and the selectivity that he uses in determining what to report all help to bring about such assurance. The Holy Spirit was using Luke's superb personality, vocabulary, and style to the hilt as He inspired his writings.

The account of the miracles in chapter three ought to astound us as much as it did those who knew the healed cripple. People, lame from birth, do not, upon a spoken word, rise from their seat, jumping and walking, completely healed—unless they are healed miraculously. Here is a further assurance for the faith of Christians. That surely was one of the reasons Luke recounts this event for Theophilus (and why God moved him to record it for you).

But there is more. Notice how Peter removes any and all credit for the miracle from himself. He places Jesus Christ front and center. It is *His* Name that He stresses. This is so important in our day of groupie and celebrity thinking. Too many people are developing "ministries" with their own names attached to them. Too many Christians are devoted not to biblical truth that is taught to them, but to the persons who teach these truths. It is time that all Christians examine their emphasis; is it upon themselves or upon Jesus Christ? Verses 12 and 16 indicate the proper way to address the blessings that others receive through one's ministry.

The boldness of speech that characterized Peter's address is also instructive. In verses 13 through 15, he tells it like it is, even to the point of calling his listeners murderers! How often Christians are afraid that if they speak the truth, they will get into trouble! Of course, that is precisely what happened to Peter and John (Acts 4:1-2). But something else also happened: 5,000 men believed (Acts 4:3-4; we have no count of the women or children who believed)! Is it worth the results to step forward in the Name of Christ to present the gospel to the unsaved as Peter did? It certainly seems so; God blessed his courage. Yet He doesn't promise that thousands will be saved.

Notice also how prominently Peter set forth the Old Testament Scriptures in discussing this incident (vv. 22-26). The *experience* is verified by the *Word*. The Word of God was plainly taught; there was no reliance upon the miracle alone. And that Word was exegeted and applied, as you can see from a simple perusal of this section. Note as well that the direct, personal application in the second person runs all through what Peter said to the people. It is "you, you, you," not "we, we, we," as so many preachers have learned to say.

So there is much in this narrative that shows in part how the gospel went from Jerusalem to Rome. It is certain that it was by preaching a plain, straightforward message, adapted to each group,[6] that the world of the day heard the message.

Drawing the truth and principles for living from a passage is not dependent on the miraculous element therein. But the original miracle-studded narrative has meaning for us today from the standpoint that we, too, need to see how God authenticated His Son and those whom He sent out as His ambassadors. Learn to use passages that contain the miraculous for both purposes.

---

6   With Jews, the speaker uses Scripture as his authority. Later on with the Gentiles it becomes clear that the same scriptural message is taught, though the Bible is not referred to since it held no authority for them. The Jew also could see that the cross was no mishap; by quoting Old Testament prophecies, the speaker could demonstrate that God's plan was being carried out fully.

CHAPTER 9

SEEKING A SIGN

THERE is no question about the problem; Paul put it this way, "the Jews ask for signs …" (1 Corinthians 1:22). That is an interesting observation. The Jew's mentality in Paul's day was that the sign was all-important. As Paul saw it, this demand for a sign characterized the Jew as much as any other factor.[7] Apart from the sign, the Jew would not believe.[8] His faith was centered in the sign. The Jews of Paul's day rejected the Lord Jesus because He refused to provide the kind of sign that they desired. Jesus Himself analyzed and explained that mentality. Something of the same mentality exists among those who claim to have special, extraordinary gifts today. The average charismatic of our time seeks out the teacher, healer, or exorcist[9] who can "perform." That leader's performance is what attracts and holds him. It is not, fundamentally, the leader's teaching (except, perhaps, teaching about gifts, signs, and wonders). We can respond to this need for signs today, just as Jesus responded to their desires for "a sign from the heavens."

Let's take a look at some of the passages in which Jesus addressed the matter. On occasion after occasion, the leaders of the nation demanded a sign from Jesus. When Jesus cleansed the temple, for instance, they came to Him asking, "What sign are you going to show us to back up your actions?" (John 2:18). On the surface, this request sounds reasonable enough. But how did Jesus respond to

---

7   As a former member of the Sanhedrin Paul, of all persons, should know!
8   Jesus performed many signs; why, then, was it that the Jews did not turn to Him in droves? We shall examine this matter further on in the chapter.
9   Some churches so define themselves by the particular sign-gifts that they profess to have that they put such things in their names. Those, for instance, that call themselves "deliverance" churches show that their concern is for what is often called "spiritual warfare," otherwise known as casting out demons.

their request? He said, "Destroy this temple and in three days I will raise it again" (v. 19). What did He mean by that, and how was His reply an answer to their demand?

The apostle John goes on to explain that "He was speaking about His body as a temple" (v. 21), and notes that when He was raised from the dead, His disciples remembered that He had said this, "and they believed the Scriptures and Jesus' word" (v. 22). Clearly, the sign He would give (elsewhere described as the sign of Jonah)[10] had the proper effect upon those who had a heart to believe the Scriptures and His word. Indeed, even the other earthly signs that had been rejected as inadequate by the religious leaders were satisfactory for those crowds of people who had been prepared by John the Baptist for His coming. As we shall see, those who did not pay attention to the Scriptures would not believe even when He rose from the dead.[11]

Later, John records a similar request from the unbelieving Jews: "What sign are you going to perform then, that we may see and believe you?" (John 6:30).[12] They then refer to Moses' giving of the manna in the wilderness, stressing that the bread came "from heaven" (v. 31). Again, Jesus' reply was enigmatical. He referred to *Himself* again, this time describing Himself as the *"true* Bread from *heaven"* (v. 32), and then said, "even though you have seen Me you won't believe" (v. 36). In other words, He Himself was the sign (the Bread) from heaven that they said they sought. They asked for a sign to "see"; but, as He told them, to "see" *Him* was enough, because He *was*, in His life and ministry, the sign that God sent. There could be no greater sign than that Emmanuel had come: in Christ, *God* Himself was *with* them!

Jesus went on to discourse upon the need to eat *Him* as the Bread that God gave them from the heavens (v. 51-57). But many

---

10   Matthew 12:39ff.
11   As He predicted in Luke 16:29-31.
12   Imagine this happening just after witnessing the miraculous feeding of the crowd (John 6:1-13)! The people whose hearts were open to the truth, however, believed (John 6:14).

stumbled over this saying (v. 61). So He explained that it was not His physical body to which He referred but to His "words" that, if believed, would give them eternal life (v. 63). Jesus described Himself as the sign that God had sent them from heaven. They needed no other sign than the person He was and the teachings that He set forth.

That is not to say that Jesus did no signs. The Scriptures are replete with records of the signs and wonders that were wrought by Him. People were healed, demons were cast out, and the dead were raised. Indeed, the book of John itself is a book of signs.[13] As John wrote, in summarizing the Gospel,

> *Jesus did many other signs in the disciples' presence that aren't written in this book, but these are written so that you may believe that Jesus is the Christ, God's Son, and that by believing you may have eternal life in His name.*

> *(John 20:30-31)*

Therefore, there is no question that, as Peter said in Acts 2:22, the signs that Jesus did "attested" to His authenticity as the Messiah of Old Testament prophecy. The signs helped the disciples and others to believe. Do we have a contradiction, then? Is it possible that Jesus and Peter disagree? Again, is John right and Jesus wrong? Is it the other way around? Or is it possible that in some way both Jesus *and* the apostles are correct? Did He do multiple signs, yet refuse to give the Pharisees a sign? Obviously, if we believe the Scriptures to be the inerrant Word of God, we must believe that both things are true. But, if so, how can that be?

Notice that Jesus' signs *did* carry authority for those who had the hearts to believe. The signs were performed in the "disciples' presence." Throughout his Gospel, John notes how after a sign was given the disciples "believed" (cf. John 2:11). Moreover, the Gospel of John was written to persons who genuinely wanted to "know" whether or not Jesus was the Messiah (John 20:30-31). But to "an

---

13   John uses the word "sign" rather than any other because of his theological emphasis on the ministry of Christ. He stresses the purpose of the wondrous works that Jesus did, rather than their nature or effect.

evil and adulterous generation," Jesus said, "no sign will be given …
except the sign of Jonah"[14] (Matthew 16:4). The fact is, then, that
Jesus did do signs and wonders. How can it be, then, that Jesus said
that no sign would be given to "this evil generation," when all along
He was doing miracles as signs in its midst?

When Jesus said that, He was speaking of *a certain kind* of sign, as
were the Scribes and the Pharisees who asked for it. The discussion
did not focus on signs in general. The religious leaders were well
aware of the miracles that Jesus did. They were simply dissatisfied
with them; they did not fit their specifications. They believed that,
as Deuteronomy 13 says, earthly signs could be falsely given—
trumped up, if you will. By their insistence on nothing less than a
sign that could not be falsified, they were virtually accusing Him
of fraud. What they wanted was an *unmistakable* sign—one that
came *from heaven* (Luke 11:16; i.e., *directly* from God the Father).
Something like the manna or fire falling from the sky in response
to Elijah's prayer is what they had in mind. It was this kind of sign
that Jesus refused to provide for them.

Notice how they spoke of the sign of the miraculous manna,
quoting the Old Testament account: "He gave them bread *from
heaven* to eat." Add to this the passages in Matthew 16:1: "The
Pharisees and Sadducees came testing Him, asking Him to show
them *a sign from heaven*," and Luke 11:16, "Others tested Him,
asking Him for a *sign from heaven*."

Again, He *was* the sign that came down from heaven. He was
literally sent by God (John 6:38). When He said that He would
ascend again into heaven (John 6:62),[15] he was thinking in terms
of the resurrection from the dead to which He alluded in His comments elsewhere about the "sign of Jonah."

Moreover, Jesus declared, "At that time the sign of the Son of
Man will appear in heaven … and they will see the Son of Man

---

14   His resurrection from the dead.
15   The sign was, in fact, a double sign: not only was He was not only the
bread *from* heaven, but also He was the One Who would also return *to* the
heaven from which He came!

coming on the clouds of heaven with power and much glory." (Matthew 24:30). All of these passages are explicit: the sign of Jonah (three days and nights in the heart of the earth), the raising of the temple (Jesus' body raised from the dead) in three days after it was destroyed, and the sign of Jesus ascended and crowned with glory, honor and power, all refer to the same complex of events. These are the events that we have been dealing with all along— the only sign that Jesus would give to that evil and adulterous generation. That is to say, the resurrection and ascension was the only sign *of the sort that they required*—a heavenly sign—that He would grant them.

Why did Jesus call His generation an "evil and adulterous" generation? Why did He call that generation "twisted"?[1] Because it was the generation that filled up the cup of the wrath of God. Previous generations had contributed to the ultimate destruction of the nation in 70 AD by their apostasy and by their killing of the prophets of God (Matthew 23:29-32). This generation would complete the cumulative process of gross degeneration that had begun in prior generations (Matthew 23:31-34). It would undertake the dubious task of filling up "the measure of the fathers' iniquity" (v. 32). This task they climaxed by committing the most audacious act of sacrilege in history—putting to death God's own Son, their Messiah![2] As a result, God would bring judgment upon that generation (vv. 35-36).[3] It was "wicked" because it determined to set its own standard of which miracles it would accept and which ones it would reject. It was a generation that attempted to tell God how to do His work! Jesus would have no part of this sinful autonomy. So he characterized the generation for what it was—wicked (twisted).[4]

Jesus called His generation "adulterous" because, as we see in many passages, the covenant between Israel and God was viewed

---

1   Or "perverse" in the King James Version. Cf. Matthew 17:17; Acts 2:40.
2   See the parables of the vineyard and the feast.
3   Note: "all these things will come upon this generation."
4   A generation that, if it could, would twist God's ways to conform to its own.

as a marriage contract. When Israel went after other gods, it was considered an act of spiritual adultery (cf. Jeremiah 3:20; 31:32; Isaiah 57:3; Hosea 3:1; Ezekiel 16:15). Anything that any person raises above God is his idol. He is therefore considered adulterous in God's sight when he lives for that idol. James even calls nominal Christians "adulteresses" because of their friendship with the world. They loved the world and the things in the world, rather than cultivating a friendship with God (James 4:4). Today, that sort of spiritual adultery is rife in the church. Many so-called Christians seem to have set themselves against God as His "enemies."

Unlike the majority of his associates, Nicodemus (who came ultimately to believe) was a man who *could* appreciate the signs that Jesus did. He did not ask for a sign from the heavens; he was already captivated by those signs that convinced the disciples. Unlike his associates, he took Jesus on His own terms. Here is what he said: "Rabbi, we know that you are a teacher who has come from God because nobody can do these signs that you are doing unless God is with him."[5] He did not demand a heavenly sign as others did.

The earthly signs that Jesus did were quite adequate to attest to His divinity for those who had the hearts to believe, even though they did not convince the rulers who had no desire to see Jesus change the status quo. The Scribes and Pharisees laid down their own terms (nothing but a sign from heaven will do) and expected Jesus to conform to them. Jesus, in contrast, set forth His terms and expected *them* to conform!

Now, we will consider once more the passage in Deuteronomy 13 that we looked at earlier. A true prophet would not only work wonders, but he would also teach the truth. The emphasis falls precisely upon Jesus' Word in the discussions with the religious rulers. After debating the matter of signs, to which we referred in John

---

5   Nicodemus later was seen defending Jesus (John 7:50-52), and still later appearing (John 19:39) at the tomb when others had fled. There seems to have been a progression in his faith. Unlike other Pharisees, Nicodemus came to get the facts and examined them. He considered the evidence from the acts and words of Jesus fairly, unlike those who were blinded by thick prejudice.

6, Jesus concluded the discussion by saying, "If you had believed Moses, you would have believed Me, because he wrote about Me. So if you don't believe his writings, how are you going to believe Me?" (John 5:46-47). The test of a prophet was not—remember— miracles alone,[6] but miracles accompanied by true teaching about God. The teaching was uppermost. The rulers had either ignored that aspect of the test or had forgotten it. And remember also, the test of doctrine was to outweigh the test of the fulfillment of the miracle. Of the two, it was to be the determining factor.

Clearly, this was the central problem. Jesus was performing miracles to call attention to the fact that the Messiah had come and teaching the people the truth of God—the truth that leads to salvation. He pointed regularly to the prophecy of Daniel as proof that He was all that He claimed to be. Yet, the religious rulers failed to take Him seriously.

If you want to know what Jesus' ministry was all about, there you have it in a nutshell: performing wonders and teaching. Jesus' teaching was rejected by the Pharisees, who had placed their own theology above that which was taught in the Scriptures. They had actually made the Word of God "of no effect" in the eyes of the people by the traditions in which they encased it (Matthew 15:6). The Sermon on the Mount, which exposed the error of these tra- ditionalists, must have turned them off early on. Jesus' teaching was at odds with them at every point. Yet it was such teaching that authenticated His signs and wonders. They were mainly concerned about outward conformity to the traditions of the elders, whereas Jesus preached inner (heart) conformity to the Bible (cf. Matthew 15:7-20). Jesus upheld and fulfilled the law, while they "relaxed" it. They could read the "signs" of the "weather," but they could not read the "signs of the times." The minds of the rulers were closed to the words of the Lord Jesus, because they refused to abandon their hypocritical ways. All who were open to His words, seemed also to be open to His signs.

---

6   And nothing was said about miracles from *heaven*.

This dynamic is also seen in the words of the Lord as He told the parable of the rich man and Lazarus (Luke 16:19-31). The rich man, suffering in hell, implores Abraham to send Lazarus from the dead to his brothers so they will believe. Abraham's reply is instructive: "They have Moses and the Prophets;[7] let them listen to them" (v. 29). The rich man then says, "But if somebody from the dead goes to them, they will repent" (v. 30). But as He continues the parable, Jesus clinches the matter with this telling response: "If they won't listen to Moses and the Prophets, they won't be persuaded even if somebody rises from the dead" (v. 31). And when He did, of course, they weren't! That Jesus would give the Pharisees and the Sadducees no other sign than His resurrection and heavenly coronation in heaven, they for the most part remained unbelieving.

Now, what does all of this have to do with signs and wonders today? There are people whose faith rests solely upon the supposed signs and wonders that are worked by modern-day charismatics. If the leaders who perform these "miracles" show their feet of clay, either by running off with the funds—or with the secretary—the people's faith falls flat. That is because they depend on men and what they can *do*, without examining carefully the doctrines that they *teach*. They commit the fallacy of the Jewish religious rulers: they forget that the test of Deuteronomy 13 is *twofold*. In particular, they fail to recognize that doctrine outweighs signs. It is only when *both* are in full accord with the teaching of the Bible that one may accept a prophet as valid.

Most of those who adhere to the views of the Pentecostal and charismatic churches would not do so apart from what they perceive to be tongues and other supposed signs. The churches in question would have little appeal otherwise. They appeal to those who seek a sign. These churches certainly are not renowned for solid, exegetical teaching of the Word. If anything, their teaching "ministries" are extremely thin. But they have the attraction of emotion, healings, and other sorts of supposed miraculous gifts. Superficial faith rests upon a superficial foundation.

---

7   A phrase that meant the Scriptures of the Old Testament.

Our generation, in many ways, is greatly dissimilar to the apostolic age, as I have pointed out in an earlier chapter. But, sadly, there seems to be one way in which our generation is becoming like the generation during the apostolic age. Our generation's churches are failing to trust God's Word for the guidance and revelation that it is intended to provide. As a consequence, our generation of professed Christians seems increasingly to run after signs. The charismatic movement has grown rapidly and is now sprawling all over the world because many are attracted to the claims of professional sign workers. The larger the following, the more our generation looks like the generation of Christ's day—it is becoming a sign-seeking generation. People prefer to seek signs rather than to search the Scripture.

Ignorance of the Bible and dependence upon emotional factors (like supposed revelation through sensings, nudgings, feelings, promptings, and checks in the spirit, along with the claim of direct revelation in dreams, in visions, and by voices) seem to be the order of the day.[8] The church is fast becoming another Montanus movement.[9] Those who engage in these activities are willing to rest their faith on supposed "partial" revelation akin to that which ceased long ago with the death of the apostles and those to whom they granted extraordinary revelatory gifts. They settle for the uncertain when they can have the sure. They try to eke out a life, living according to that which is seen but dimly as if in a bronze mirror, rather than living based on the ability to see clearly as one does face to face. It makes no sense to prefer the dubious over the certain—simply on the gamble that there may be something to the charismatic sign approach after all. When God has said in no uncertain terms that tongues have ceased and that prophecy and special knowledge have been set aside, what are people doing when they attempt to activate these gifts? They are tempting God.[10]

---

8   See my book *The Christian's Guide to Guidance*.
9   Perhaps the earliest evidence of the supposed use of extraordinary gifts in church history. The group became heretical.
10   There is no need to explain the phenomena that take place in charismatic

Nothing could be more important in our day than for people to turn back to Moses and the Prophets. If and when they do, their faith will be centered in the One Who Himself is *the* sign from the heavens, rather than in works which were intended only to point to Him. There is no need for miracles today; Jesus' death and resurrection for sinners is well-attested to, not only by the signs He did along the way, but also preeminently by the great sign of the resurrected Son of Man—God in human flesh—seated on the heavenly throne at the Father's right hand.

People who look for signs come perilously close to requiring God to operate according to their preconceived programs. They are asking God to jump through their hoops. In this, they are like the Pharisees. It was that mentality which drove the evil, adulterous generation, of which Jesus spoke so vehemently. It was (and ours is becoming) a generation that insisted on and practiced its own way of doing things—regardless! That can readily turn into adulterous idolatry. It is always dangerous to demand from God what He has said He will not give.

---

meetings as either deceitful, self-delusive or demonic. The issue is simply this: however it may be explained, it is wrong—biblically. And that ought to be enough.

SINCE I have spent a significant amount of time discussing what the Holy Spirit does not do among our churches, it is only right that I should focus for at least a short time on what He *does* do. But first, let's summarize a bit of what we have learned so far.

In our time, the Holy Spirit does not raise up prophets (people with supernaturally given knowledge) or those who speak in tongues (without having studied the language). Paul told us that these gifts of the Spirit would come to an end—and they did! At the end of the "last days" (which were concluded in 70 AD, or thereabouts), the offices of apostle and prophet were discontinued because they were no longer needed. Christ gave them as "foundational" gifts to His church, distributing them through the Holy Spirit, Whom He sent from heaven upon His ascension and coronation. These gifts the apostles faithfully used to found the church which, according to Paul's letter to the Colossians, had been spread abroad among all the nations of the day. The usefulness of the signs and wonders from the Spirit had come to an end. The apostles and the prophets completed God's written revelation, and there was no longer a need to attest to its divine origin as there had been at the beginning.

We, in our time, must build upon the foundation of the apostles and the prophets. As a significant part of their foundational work, they worked signs and wonders, and gave and received special revelation in bits and pieces. They also communicated, by the laying on of hands, some of these powers to others in churches that they established. This was to enable these congregations to learn God's will about various matters when they were not present.[1] Moreover, since "that which was complete"—the written books that we call the New Testament—had not yet come, this was the only way for them during the transitional apostolic age to do so. However, the major revelatory task of the apostles and the prophets, that the Spirit superintended, was to produce and disseminate God's Word to His people in a completed, written form. This was accomplished by the end of their lives. Thus, by means of the efforts of the apostles in whom He worked to bring it about, the Spirit fulfilled Jesus' promise in John 14:26.

We saw, also, that in order to attest their mission from God, the Spirit worked miracles by their hands. Since there are no more apostles, and since revelation is complete, authenticating signs and wonders no longer happen. If signs took place today, we would have to search for the person or persons that they would authenticate, and we would expect them to reveal inspired truth in addition to a *completed* canon—which, of course, would be a contradiction.[2] If there are no apostles to whom such signs attest, then what would be their purpose? Yet, contrary to all reason, some maintain that the Holy Spirit continues to provide sign gifts. But there could be no "signs of a true apostle" where there are no apostles!

"Well," you say, "if all that is so, what is it that the Spirit does today?"

A good question—that deserves a good answer. Since the revelatory gifts of the Spirit ceased with the end of the apostolic age, we dare not arrogate to ourselves the promises that were made exclusively to the apostles. The Spirit fully supplied Jesus with all things necessary for His unique ministry. He supplied the apostles and the prophets with that which they needed for theirs. And He supplies you and me with all that we need for ours. What need would we have for sign gifts? We are neither Jesus nor the apostles. We have been given the Spirit for the purposes for which we need His presence and power.

---

1   Cf. Acts 8:17-18; 1 Corinthians 12-14.
2   That is so, since it would mean the canon was not complete and, therefore, not a canon.

"But what are these purposes?"

We know that the Spirit continues to do His *ordinary* work. That is because these are ordinary times. Today, there is nothing going on that is like the breaking in on the kingdom of darkness—as there was in the time of Jesus, Who remarked that the result of His work was like Satan's falling from heaven (Luke 10:18)! Nor is there anything like the foundational ministry of the apostles during our time. Nothing extraordinary was either predicted or is happening that would call for something more from the Spirit than His ordinary work.

That ordinary work, of course, consists of His regenerating and His sanctifying work. *That* is what the Spirit is up to today. He gives life to those who are dead in trespasses and sins (Cf. Ephesians 2:5) so that they may believe the gospel. He is a "life-giving Spirit" (1 Corinthians 15:45). Then, having drawn men to Christ in saving faith, He indwells them and enables them to love God and their neighbor as they were unable to do in the past (Romans 5:5). In bringing this about, He busily fights the flesh, in the place of which He plants His fruit, then cultivates it, bringing it to bud and finally to flower (Galatians 5:22ff.). This work is a lifelong work—one that He never completes in this world.

Furthermore, as a part of that sanctifying task, the Spirit enables the regenerate believer to understand and appropriate the teachings that He has inspired in the Bible. In other words, the Spirit *uses* the Word that He produced! He illumines believers (i.e., enables them to understand what He has caused to be written).[3] This illuminating task is an essential element in His sanctifying work. When Jesus prayed for the disciples' sanctification, He declared that sanctification takes place by the application of God's Word:

Sanctify them by the truth; Your word is truth!

(John 17:17)

Compare that verse with 1 Corinthians 2, where it is clear that only the "spiritual person" (i.e., one who has the Spirit dwelling in

---

3   Cf. 1 Corinthians 2:9-16.

him) can understand the things of God's Word (which are called there the "teachings of God's Spirit" (v. 14), and you will see something of how it all comes together. The Spirit's "teachings" were given through the apostolic writers who, under His divine inspiration, penned inerrant words that were equally theirs and His; the Spirit also indwells those to whom these writings were directed, so that they might understand, believe, and live according to them. That is how He fights against the flesh[4] and produces fruit.

Moreover, it is by His power that the Spirit enables the believer to do those things that please God. Listen to 1 Peter 1:2, where Peter says: "that by the Spirit's sanctification you may obey." By His Spirit, Paul says, "it is God Who is producing in you both the willingness and the ability to do the things that please Him" (Philippians 2:13). The Spirit took thousands of years to complete the Bible. He did so, not to ignore it, but in order to use it in sanctifying God's people. In Romans 15:13, for instance, Paul shows that the Holy Spirit produces hope in the believer. But according to verse 4 of that same chapter, it is clear that He does so by the encouragement that the Scriptures give:

> *Whatever was written before was written for our instruction, that by the endurance and the encouragement that the Scriptures give us we may have hope.*
>
> *(Romans 15:4)*

Surely, then, the Spirit is busy today. In putting aside His extraordinary work and concentrating on His ordinary work, the Holy Spirit is still actively at work in the world. Some seem to forget this all-important fact. One cannot help but wonder how those who so stress the spectacular can also place enough emphasis on the ordinary, crucial work of sanctification.

There are other works of the Spirit in our time. He is the down payment and seal of our salvation (Ephesians 1:13-14).[5] Paul alludes

---

4   For information on the "flesh," see my book *Winning the War Within.* Biblically speaking, flesh means *the body wrongly habituated by the sinful nature with which one is born.* The flesh and the Satanic powers must be fought by using the "sword of the Spirit" (Ephesians 6:17).
5   His presence is evidence that we belong to God.

to this also in Romans 8:16, where he says that "the Spirit Him-self testifies together with [not "to"][6] our spirit that we are God's children."

As He did in the many non-extraordinary times in the Old Testament (the periods of the miraculous were also brief periods of revelation) and during the inter-testamental period of 400 years, the Spirit does only the ordinary today. He silently, but powerfully, goes about His works of regeneration, witness, and sanctification.[7] It is entirely wrong for people to demand more of Him. He is doing what He led us to believe He would do in the Bible. What is inferior about any of these activities of the Spirit? They all lead to edification—that which Paul, when writing to the Corinthian church, singled out as more important than the spectacular gifts (see the argument in 1 Corinthians 14). It is interesting that this very carnal church at Corinth was all caught up in the more showy, rather than the sanctifying, elements of the Spirit's work. That is sometimes true today about those who emphasize the same thing: their sanctification seems to lag sadly behind. The mentality that seeks the miraculous may account for this! Remembering the way Jesus characterized His sign-seeking generation seems to lead to such a conclusion.

Thus, as always, the Spirit carries on His works of regeneration and sanctification. Only ingrates expect more of Him. We must, therefore, not only be grateful for these important works of the Spirit, but also rejoice in the fact that God has so provided for us. Let us not be unthankful, demanding more than is our right, but instead prayerfully submit with glad hearts to what the Spirit will do for us.

---

6   The idea here is of two witnesses: the internal witness of our own con-science and the external witness of the Spirit in the Word. The Greek word translated "together with" in Romans 8:16 is *sun*.
7   This also includes His help in prayer (cf. Romans 8:26-27; Ephesians 6:18; Jude 20).

CHAPTER 11

WHAT *IS* WRONG WITH THE CHURCH?

JIM CYMBALA'S book is a challenge to all Bible believing, conservative churches. They are failing, he believes, because of their lack of the direct work of the Holy Spirit among them. He says that this lack can be traced back to the lack of adequate prayer. According to Cymbala, when people don't ask for the blessing of God, they don't receive it. In his own congregation, people pray around the clock, seven days a week. And there are times when preaching is either set aside completely or it is greatly shortened in favor of prayer. Prayer is Cymbala's panacea. He says, "We must face the fact that for our churches and ministries to be all that God wants them to be, they *must* be saturated with prayer."[1]

While few would disagree with the thesis that prayer is important, and most of us would confess that we pray too infrequently and often ineffectively, we must ask whether Cymbala has put his finger on the central problem in the church. That the church is weak—far weaker than it ought to be given the number of attendees and the amounts of money, time, and labor expended—no one who knows the church today can refute. But, again, is Cymbala right? Indeed, it is important even to ask, "Is there only one problem as he supposes? Or is the matter more complex?" I want to sketch what I believe makes the issue far more complex, while at the same time disclosing a common thread in all of the elements that contribute to the weakened condition of the church in this land.

It is my contention that Cymbala and others who follow his line oversimplified the problem; moreover, their approach has contributed to the difficulties in which many churches find themselves today.

---

1   *Op. cit.,* p. 183.

The confusion that is in the church in many quarters is, in no small measure, due to the imprecise and downright erroneous ways in which the faith is conceived and propagated. As we consider this matter, you will see what I mean. Remember, God put teaching first.

There is *not* one cause for the weakness of the church, considered as the proximate reason for this weakness. There are many proximate causes. A number of factors simultaneously weaken the church. In this chapter, I shall mention roughly a half dozen, though they often are combined into several stews of various flavors. All of these, in one way or another, impinge on the church from various sides.

Consider, for instance, liberalism. During the late 1800s and early 1900s, the liberals began to take over the mainline churches. By the 1940s, they were firmly entrenched in virtually all of them. They held key administrative positions, owned the seminaries and the publishing houses, and—through the Federal Council of Churches (precursor to the National Council of Churches)—had exclusive control of the airwaves. Conservatives, who had either been silenced or left by the wayside, were hanging on by their toenails. Those who did not compromise by remaining in increasingly apostate denominations struggled outside in storefront assemblies without funds or clout in the community. In time, God blessed their faithfulness, increased their numbers and funds, and eventually turned the tables on the liberals. Now, half a century later, it is the Bible-believing churches that are in the ascendancy, while liberals are losing members, money, and munitions.

But the effects of liberalism have not been totally erased. They have instead been widespread and continue to exert much influence—even upon conservative churches. Many of the ideas floated by liberals have remained in the general culture. For example, the fundamental attack on the validity and authority of the Scriptures led directly to the cultural revolution of the fifties and the sixties. In that revolution, all authority in society was challenged. But where God's fundamental authority in the Bible is weakened, all other authority is weakened as well. So today, in the aftermath of that revolution, the sixties generation is in the saddle of the country and of the church, and the authority of the state, the school, the home, *and* the church is so weakened that, in some instances, it hardly exists. Even in Bible-believing churches, people have imbibed these anti-authority sentiments, to the weakening of the pulpit (people pick and choose what they will believe and how they will live) and the weakening of the eldership as well. As evidence, consider the widespread refusal of conservative churches to teach and practice church discipline.

Along with the demise of church authority, there also came in the wake of the sixties the ascendancy of lay leadership in the church. While there may have been too much prelacy[2] before, the reaction to the liberal prelates in the pulpits was the conservative laymen's seizing of the control of the teaching and leadership functions of large portions of the church. Their reaction to the liberals, and to the compromising ministers who ought to have fought liberalism themselves, caused many to turn against denominations and organized Christianity of every sort. Para-church organizations, headed by charismatic and influential laymen, sprang up in place of these. Instead of the honored place they once had in society, ministers were made into a laughing stock in the movies and on television. Many who despised the capitulation of a goodly number of conservatives joined in the derision. Darbyism declared the church a net full of bad fish, and there were many who agreed. So the organized church herself came into disfavor—even with many of those who should have defended and strengthened her in her hour of trial.

These influential, liberated laymen, because they had access to wealth that the struggling conservative ministers in the storefronts lacked, began to purchase radio and (later) TV time. By these means, and the dissemination of literature, they soon became the conservative gurus who could readily outshine the local pastor. Congregational members listened to them day after day. Many local pastors soon discovered that they could not compete. The radio-TV speaker had the ear of his listeners five days a week—usually for the

---

2   An exclusive rule by the clergy, with the lay members merely as spectators.

better part of an hour. In contrast, the preacher on Sunday commanded only one-half an hour one day a week. If and when the pastor disagreed with the celebrity on the airwaves, he would often be disparaged as unacquainted with the truth (or worse). Yet, many (probably most) of these celebrity preachers, psychologists, and the like, never had any training like that of the local pastor. The latter would be acquainted with the Greek and Hebrew and use good commentaries. The former often "winged it" with superficial and erroneous teaching. Principally, they succeeded because they were glib. Over time, the celebrity overwhelmed the pastor, as day after day he drummed his superficial and/or erroneous messages into itching ears.

Talk show hosts on "Christian" TV networks gave their often quite erroneous opinions about every subject under the sun. Not to be outdone, the "Christian" psychologists and psychiatrists, many of whom admit they are not theologians, joined the parade, adding their particular nostrums. They pontificated on marriage problems, how to train and deal with youth, and every sort of life problem in the book. Yet, much of what they had to say was at odds with the Scriptures. Moreover, these men (and women) soon found their way into the seminaries, as well as the Christian colleges and universities: in these institutions, they have trained a couple of generations of Christian graduates in the ways of Freud, Rogers, and the other pagans—whose philosophies and systems they so easily adopted. After they unwittingly learned what these so-called "authorities" taught in "Christian" institutions, graduates flooded into the conservative churches which, as a result, quickly became psychologized.

In addition to this, what has become known as "Neo-evangelicalism" raised its head within the ranks of conservative churches and educational institutions. Purporting to believe in the inerrancy of the Scriptures, Neo-evangelicals undercut much biblical teaching by their use of semi-liberal and neo-orthodox approaches to the text. The introduction of form-criticism[3] and other higher critical notions

---

3   The view that much biblical material is just "forms," not historical fact.

into formerly conservative circles, for instance, has contributed to a breakdown of faith in the trustworthiness of the Bible.

Moreover, a biblical-theological overemphasis in preaching, in which neatly-woven essays are substituted for exposition and exhortation, has likewise weakened many conservative congregations' grip on biblical truth. In addition, preachers who attempt this sort of "preaching" often wind up saying little more than the same thing week after week, as they attempt to emulate their professors. Talks that professors put together over many weeks of study are hardly the sort of fare that the twice-weekly preacher is able to duplicate—if even he should. The idea is strikingly unrealistic. Indeed, there is a sense of unreality about the entire business.

This biblical-theological overemphasis has another dimension. Meredith Kline's pan-covenantalism, by which he casts the entire Bible into the mold of the suzerain-servant relationship found in Near Eastern peoples, has had its toll.[4] Kline's system is so intricate that one person who ceased attending his classes said, "If people had to understand such convoluted teachings in order to interpret his Bible, then no normal person could do so." Eggheadism has contributed its share of difficulty.

So the choice for the average church member seems to be between the superficial mouthings of would-be leaders of the church, who do very little exegesis, and the "experts" who spin theories so complicated that they undermine simple interpretation. Some choice! Neither option is acceptable. Those who attend those few churches where the truth is still proclaimed by faithful, expository ministers are especially blessed in times like these.

Now, add to the mix the "seeker sensitive" and "church growth" people who survey the community to discover what it is that people prefer in a church (rather than determine what God prefers!). As a result of their surveys, they offer "Christianity lite." They soft-pedal

---

For instance, the coming of the wise men is said not to be an historical event, but simply a form used to herald the coming of Gentiles into the church.
4   Again and again the liberal Mendenhall is cited in the footnotes of his books, showing the direction in which Kline is inclined.

repentance, judgment, and other "hard" teachings of the Bible that John the Baptist, Jesus, and Paul taught. Accordingly, the faith of the people they attract can only be suspect. Doubtless, many remain unconverted. At best, they can do little more than adhere to a "lite theology."

Eclectics of every kind abound. There are those who adopt psychological, sociological, business, and marketing views and practices, baptizing these into the Christian faith unconverted. These techniques further dilute the Scriptural message. This unholy mix weakens those who drink deeply of it. Close to this problem is worldliness—the penchant for thinking and acting as unbelievers do. Many eclectics—especially in educational institutions—snuggle up to pagans in order to gain respect. They seek their approval, but rarely achieve it. Indeed, some of these intellectuals seem much more concerned about what unbelievers think than what God thinks.

Finally, there are the charismatics. Their focus usually is on the spectacular, the emotional, and the pseudo-spiritual.[5] They think that unless the extraordinary is present in a congregation it is spiritually bereft. So much for the quiet life of solid, steady Christian living! Teaching (other than that which has to do with spiritual gifts) is downplayed in favor of something else. In Cymbala's case, prayer is far more important than teaching. Why he, or anyone else, should suppose that man's addressing God (in prayer) is more vital than God's addressing man (in the Bible) is incomprehensible. Isn't what God has to say of much greater significance? Yet, Cymbala reports that prayer is sometimes even substituted for preaching at his church.

All of these losses that the church has sustained in this century, Cymbala rightly surmises, are due to a lack of the Spirit's power. But quite contrary to what he thinks, the losses stem mainly from loss of faith in (or use of) the Scriptures. The Spirit works through the

---

5   Notice Cymbala's exaltation of prayer over teaching as more vital and spiritual.

Word that He produced over the centuries—not apart from it. All of the various groups that I have mentioned in passing have one thing in common: in one way or another they minimize the Scriptures or replace them with something else. To the extent that the Word of God is de-emphasized, the power of God in a congregation lessens. It does not take very long, as the New Testament letters indicate, for weakened (or even false) teaching to displace the strong truths of the Bible (cf. Galatians 1:6). Cymbala is right that the church is weak and needs empowering. But that will happen only when the Bible once more is placed front and center in Christ's church.

CHAPTER 12

CONCLUSION

THE position in this book has been set forth clearly, and it has been reinforced with argument from the Scriptures. I confess, however, that it is unsupported by signs and wonders!

Without a shred of biblical evidence Cymbala says,

> I am now convinced, it is my duty and privilege, and the duty of every other Christian, to pray for as much of the Holy Spirit as came down on the day of Pentecost, and a great deal more.[6]

That statement is manifestly wrong. To begin with, who is he to think that he can have more of the Spirit than the apostles? There is that arrogance that charismatics so often exhibit once more rearing its ugly head. His sense of self-importance certainly has ballooned from his first days at the Brooklyn Tabernacle! Moreover, why would he require more of the Spirit than the apostles? He isn't writing Scripture; he isn't speaking inspired sermons; he isn't raising the dead. Why would he think that he needed an excess of the Spirit, as he says?

And how does he account for the fact that he thinks that a "great deal more" of the Spirit is *available* for him? Is there any biblical basis for such thought? Where do the Scriptures say that it is the duty of every Christian to seek this?

What I want you to see, in conclusion, is that there is a lot of pious-sounding language that is bound up in the signs and wonders approach to present-day Christianity (if it can be called such). Most of this is hollow and deceives only the uninstructed and those who are on the prowl for signs. They will not sit under a teacher who

---

6   *Op. cit.,* p. 176.

feeds them the pure meat of the Word; they prefer the (often poisoned) pabulum of the wonder-worker. Friend, if you are captivated by such matters, think again. Reread this book. Discuss it with a biblically-oriented pastor. Search the Scriptures yourself to see if these things are so. I implore you—keep your distance from signs and wonders workers. The bottom line is, you won't be disappointed if you do; you may be let down hard if you don't!

It is my sincere hope to help you see the biblical truths behind the position that I have set forth in this book. May the Lord help you to learn from the Bible one truth about signs and wonders. With it you cannot go far astray. It is this—the signs and wonders of the New Testament church were confined to the last days. The "last days" to which Joel referred ended in 70 AD. Given the completed (and complete) revelation of the New Testament, you have all you need to live as God requires you to live, serving and glorifying Him and blessing your neighbor. Be satisfied with what He has provided for you and do not long for something more!